All about the
Weimaraner

All about the Weimaraner

Patsy Hollings

PELHAM BOOKS

PELHAM BOOKS

Published by the Penguin Group
27 Wrights Lane, London W8 5TZ, England
Viking Penguin, a division of Penguin Books USA Inc
375 Hudson Street, New York, NY 10014, USA
Penguin Books Australia Ltd, Ringwood, Victoria, Australia
Penguin Books Canada Ltd, 10 Alcorn Avenue, Suite 300, Toronto, Ontario, Canada, M4V 3B2
Penguin Books (NZ) Ltd, 182–190 Wairau Road, Auckland 10, New Zealand

Penguin Books Ltd, Registered Offices: Harmondsworth, Middlesex, England

First Published 1992
1 3 5 7 9 10 8 6 4 2

Made and printed in Great Britain by
Butler & Tanner Ltd, Frome and London
Typeset in Linotron Plantin 10½/12½ pt by
Cambrian Typesetters, Frimley, Surrey

A CIP catalogue record for this book is available from the British Library.

ISBN 0 7207 1962 3
The moral right of the author has been asserted.

Photographic acknowledgements
The author and publisher are grateful to the following for permission to reproduce
copyright photographs: Keith Allison, 12, 28, 33, 36, 55, 62, 63, 65, 89, 102, 111,
112, 113, 114, 156, 165; David Dalton, 19; Dave Freeman, 11, 13, 15. Every effort
has been made to trace the copyright owners but if there have been any omissions in
this respect we apologise and will be pleased to make appropriate acknowledgement in
any further editions.

Contents

Acknowledgements

I would like to thank Eliz Wilson and Gill De Sousa for their help; Gwen Sowersby for her contribution to the Working Trials chapter; and Ann Janson for allowing me to use her article on the long-haired Weimaraner.

Preface

I have taken pleasure in the fact that during my research on Weimaraners for this book I have come across so many owners and dogs who have contributed so much to promoting this breed in all aspects of dogdom.

It is rare to find a breed so versatile that you can see dogs who have climaxed in virtually every sphere. It must account, in part, for why the breed is so popular.

One hopes that everyone captivated by the Weimaraner will work together, pooling knowledge gained by specialising in the different fields of working the dogs, so that everyone can learn and the dogs will be stimulated to their full potential by experienced or novice owners alike.

The help and information I have received during the writing of this book, willingly from all asked, has cheered me into thinking that we all will work together for the good of Weimaraners. In my opinion, it is the dogs that matter at the end of the day.

We, the owners, concern me very little. We, to a great extent, can choose our destiny, whether we marry, have children or pursue other things. However, we dictate a dog's destiny and we owe him a happy, fulfilled life. If we are not prepared for this daunting exercise we should not acquire or breed the Weimaraner in the first place. We should never discredit the breed by treating the dog as an idiot.

Remember to adore him with the respect he deserves.

1 The History of the Breed

Establishing the Breed

It is very difficult to trace the origins of the Weimaraner with accuracy. However, one assumes from the reading matter available that the Weimaraner is a very old breed.

There is a painting in Vienna by Van Dyck (*circa* 1631) of the young Prince Rupprecht Von Pfalz with a dog, remarkably similar to the Weimaraner as we know it, standing by his side.

The breed was fancied by the Grand Duke Karl August who, it is thought, brought the Weimaraner from Bohemia after he had hunted with this powerful grey dog on the estate of Prince Esterhazy and Auersperg. The Grand Duke Karl August was ruler of the state of Thuringer in East Germany in 1775. He lived in Weimar, which is now an industrial town, in the district of Erfurt.

In the 18th century Thuringer was famous for its beautiful countryside, and Weimar, where the Duke lived, was its loveliest city. It was surrounded by thick woods that were perfect for exploiting the Duke's passion for hunting. Game such as deer, boar and wild cat was thought to have been present in the woods. When the Duke discovered the intelligent, athletic, fearless grey hunting dog we know today as the Weimaraner, it is easy to see why he found this dog, with all its attributes, ideal for his use in hunting such dangerous prey.

Grand Duke Karl August was a very powerful man politically. He therefore was in a position to dictate who could have a Weimaraner. Anyone wanting these dogs had to be thoroughly vetted and approved and could only keep them as hunting dogs.

The Duke developed the breed primarily for the use of his family, his court and any passing nobility, but his breeding methods were kept a closely guarded secret. Because of the secrecy surrounding the breeding programme, details of which appear to have been lost or destroyed, not a great deal is now known about the ancestry of the Weimaraner.

The name Weimaraner obviously came from the fact that the dog was developed in Weimar, where the Duke's court produced enough dogs to establish a breed. Unfortunately, most of the history of the breed thereafter remains guess work, because records are virtually non-existent.

Sh. Ch. Ballina of Merse-
side (p. 9)

The Weimaraner's Ancestors

The German Short-haired Pointer was thought to have been introduced into the breed at some point. At first glance they appear similar, but on further inspection they differ in fundamental areas, so that idea was eventually dismissed. For instance, if you study the breed characteristics of the German Short-haired Pointer and the Weimaraner in detail, you will see the head shape and body shape differ greatly.

It was Dr Paul Kleeman, an expert on the German Short-haired Pointer, who thought the Great Dane played a part in the history of the breed, but again fundamental differences disproved that theory. The Great Dane theory probably originated with the idea that the Branchen and Schweisshund were the most logical ancestors. These being a good six inches shorter than the Weimaraner, it was thought that the Great Dane introduced the size. The Schweisshund evolved from the bloodhound family and is a branch of the St Hubertus Branchen.

Professor Lutz Heck, an authority on Branchen and a former director of the Berlin Zoo, described the Branchen as the oldest breed of hunting dog and the one from which all hunting dogs descend. In 1940 Professor Ferlringer explained that the word Branchen can be traced back to a Bishop called Branchie who lived in the 7th century. He was a hunter and was known to use dogs on the hunt. There is evidence to suggest that the Branchen may go back even further.

Ch. Gunther of Ragstone
(p. 10)

The St Hubertus Branchen is named after the monks at the Monastery of St Hubert in the Ardennes. It was thought that the dogs were sent from France to the monks of Morgan Abbey in England, and then on to Germany from France or England.

They were heavily built dogs, rather long in the body, of medium height, with excellent noses. They had power and a proven ability to hunt. They were black with red or fawn marks over their eyes, with hair of the same colour on their legs. It was said that if they had any white, it was only a small amount on their chest. This description resembles that of the Weimaraner – except for the colour – and gives rise to the speculation that the St Hubertus Branchen is the most likely ancestor of the Weimaraner.

Major Robert Der Herber, a man dedicated to the Weimaraner, nurtured the breed and helped shape it into the dog we know today. He was the President of the Weimaraner Club of Germany in 1921 and is often referred to as 'The Father of the Breed'.

He wrote: 'As the Weimaraner was not found in old literature, he did not exist as a breed.' However, such short-haired light grey dogs could well have existed in small numbers in an earlier period. They might simply have been unknown or disregarded by sports writers, whose general opinion was that they were the result of cross breeding.

As it has been proved that two black animals can produce a grey one, it seems best to look for black ancestors. One possibility is, again, the St Hubertus Branchen. The characteristics of both breeds are almost the same, so it seems possible that the Weimaraner is a mutation within the Branchen breed. The Branchen seems to be the ancestor of all Vorstenhurde, the German name for pointers. It was thought that the grey mutations were then paired and bred to produce the Weimaraner.

The Weimaraner is thought to have hound origins, owing to his incredibly good scenting ability. When he takes scent in the field, you can watch his

Ch. Wotan of Ragstone (p. 10)

Sh. Ch. Jehnvar of Greyfilk (p. 10)

instincts take over – he can be very difficult to stop. Also his looks are reminiscent of a hound.

The distinguished grey colour of the Weimaraner might also be the result of a recessive gene in the breeding of red or tan dogs. This dilutes the colour and would account for the silvery taupe of the Weimaraner coat. The Schweisshund was just such a red colour – another factor suggesting that it was one of the Weimaraner's ancestors.

Recognition of the Breed

In the 19th century fanciers of the breed tried to have it recognised and included in the Stud Book. The lack of documented records hampered this process considerably. However, the dog captured the interest of Karl Brandt, a celebrated German dog expert of the period. He and other influential men with an interest in recognising this lovely grey dog were instrumental in convincing the Delegate Commission that the Weimaraner should be included in the Stud Book.

In 1896 the Weimaraner was officially recognised as a pure breed. The Weimaraner Club of Germany was then formed a year later, with its headquarters in Thirugia. The club was initially formed by shooting men interested in working their Weimaraners as a hobby. They drew up a standard for their own interest, but the official standard of the breed was not completed and accepted until 1935. This was only accomplished through the

Ch. Ragstone Ritter (p. 10)

Sh. Ch. Monroes Nexus. A great dog behind many winners. (p. 13)

hard work of The Weimaraner Club of Germany and The Weimaraner Club of Austria.

Interest Abroad

Austria's interest had grown following Prince Hans Von Ratibor's introduction to the breed. He heard what good hunting dogs they were, and his friend Otto Von Stockmayer imported one for him from Germany. Von Ratibor eventually became President of The Weimaraner Club of Austria in 1913.

Howard Knight was responsible for introducing the Weimaraner to America. The breed first came to his attention while he was hunting with his friend Herr Grossman in Germany. He went on to join The Weimaraner Club of Germany.

Because of the very strict rules and regulations about who could own and breed the Weimaraner, he was very carefully vetted before he was allowed to export a dog and bitch to America. Unbeknownst to him, and presumably his friend, both of these dogs had been neutered. Therefore, although the breed actually arrived in America in 1929, it took Mr Knight a further nine years to convince The Weimaraner Club of Germany that he had the breed's well

Sh. Ch. Greyfilk
Knightsman (p. 13)

being at heart. They then let him have breeding stock. The bitch Aura Von Gaiberg was exported in whelp to Mr Knight. Another bitch, Dorla Von Schwarzenkamp, was accompanied by a dog, Marsaus Der Wolfsneide.

Their export was responsible for easing the strict regulations concerning the export of Weimaraners from Germany. Consequently numerous animals were exported to all corners of the world.

In 1943 the Weimaraner was officially recognised by the American Kennel Club.

Weimaraners in Britain

The breed was imported to England by Major R.H. Petty and Major Eric Richardson. They had encountered this unusual grey dual-purpose gundog while serving in the army in Germany: both were very keen shots.

Although both men were instrumental in introducing the Weimaraner to the UK, it was Major Bob Petty who was dedicated to the Weimaraner and set about researching its history. He was responsible for successfully importing the first Weimaraners to England in 1952. Cobra Von Boberstrand was the first Weimaraner bitch to step on to British soil. It is said she was very beautiful. With her was the dog Bando Von Fohr.

Mrs Olga Mallett also imported an in-whelp bitch and a dog from Germany and had two litters bearing the Ipley affix. Between the three of them – Major Petty, Major Richardson and Mrs Mallett – fifteen Weimaraners were imported into this country. However, after looking at and considering their quality, only nine were registered with The Kennel Club. Only those nine were bred from and went on to form the foundation of our Weimaraners today. I find it fascinating that those nine Weimaraners can be found in present-day pedigrees without too much effort.

Well-known Affixes

Major Richardson took the affix Monksway, but it was Major Petty's affix Strawbridge that has proved to be such an important factor in present-day Weimaraners in this country. It is fitting that the breed's first champion was a dog bearing this affix, Champion (Ch.) Strawbridge Oliver.

Another great, bearing the Strawbridge affix, was Strawbridge Carol, owned by Mr and Mrs Causely. She won Best Bitch at Crufts on four consecutive occasions, from 1955 to 1958 inclusive. Obviously she would have been Show Champion (Sh. Ch.) but The Kennel Club only granted Challenge Certificates to Weimaraners in 1960. Out of interest, four sets of C.C.s were on offer that year.

Although Oliver was bred by Major Petty, he was owned, campaigned

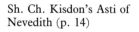

Sh. Ch. Kisdon's Asti of Nevedith (p. 14)

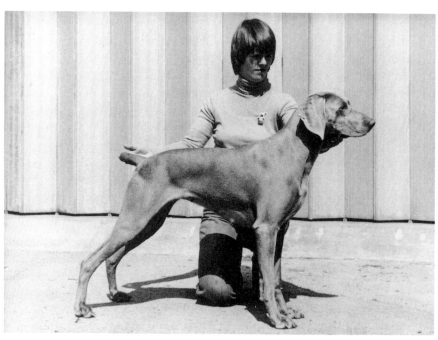

Sh. Ch. Kisdon's Derring-Do (p. 14)

and worked by Mr and Mrs Webb, whose affix was Theocsbury. This affix is behind, amongst others, Dick Finch's first Weimaraner Show Champion Hansom Syhill Odette, whose dam was Ch. Theocsbury Abbie. It is no wonder Hansom produced some really good stock when you consider that the sire of this foundation bitch was the great Ch. Ragstone Remus. Remus is in fact behind all the Ragstone stock and, of course, so many great Weimaraners.

Ragstone

Ragstone is Tony and Gillian Burgoin's affix. In 1963 they acquired Remus from Mr and Mrs Milward. He grew up to be Ch. Ragstone Remus and was, among other things – including being field qualified – the first Weimaraner to win a Junior Warrant, in 1964. A winner of sixteen Challenge Certificates (C.C.s) and three Green Stars (the Irish equivalent of a C.C.), he did much for the breed with his stud work. He was the sire of seven Champions or Show Champions, including Ch. Gunther of Ragstone, joint record holder with Sh. Ch. Ballina of Merse-side with thirty-one C.C.s.

Ballina, owned and campaigned by Mrs Elizabeth Hacket, holds the record for C.C.s won by a bitch, including twenty-nine Best of Breeds. In her first show, at six months, she won an A.V. Puppy Class of forty-six entries and went on to win Best Puppy in the Show. She won four BIS at

Open Shows, a rare achievement for a Weimaraner in those days, numerous reserve or best opposite sex in show at Open Shows and eleven Best Bitch awards at Championship Shows where C.C.s were not on offer – if they had been, she probably would have forty-two C.C.s.

Gunther was a Championship Show Group winner, campaigned by Mrs Marion Wardell and co-owned with her husband. He won Best in Show at the All Breeds Open Show and Gundog Open Shows and was six times BIS at The Weimaraner Club of Great Britain. Gunther's full litter brother Ch. Wotan of Ragstone, bred by Mrs Fearn out of the Austrian import Dinna vom Morebach, won eleven C.C.s, a Group and Best Gundog at the East of England Championship Show in 1978 for his owner Di Arrowsmith, who field qualified him. Two Group winners out of the same litter is a record not yet beaten.

Sh. Ch. Jehnvar of Greyfilk, winner of four C.C.s, was the son of Gunther out of a Greyfilk bitch, whose breeding proved a recipe for success as the sire of eight Sh. Ch. or Ch. offspring. Owned by Absalom's, he came to them as a rescue at four and a half years of age, grossly overweight. It is a credit to them that they got him into condition to gain four C.C.s.

The Burgoins took back a stud puppy by Remus, bred by Mr Modi, in the form of Ch. Ragstone Ritter. A winner of twenty-two C.C.s, he won eleven Best in Shows at Open Shows and Best Dog at Crufts for five consecutive years. He also qualified in the field. He followed in his father's footsteps by

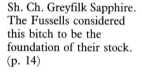

Sh. Ch. Greyfilk Sapphire. The Fussells considered this bitch to be the foundation of their stock. (p. 14)

Sh. Ch. Hansom
Brandyman of Gunalt
(p. 14)

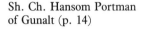

Sh. Ch. Hansom Portman
of Gunalt (p. 14)

becoming a prolific stud and helping to shape today's Weimaraners. Many
winning and good dogs in all areas of work and show go back to this great
chap.

Manana and Monroes

Manana was another early affix and belonged to Mrs Maddocks. In fact, a
bitch named Manana Athene was the foundation bitch for Mrs Douglas
Reddin's Wolfox affix. Athene's daughter, bearing this affix, became the
first Weimaraner Show Champion in this country in 1960; her name was Sh.
Ch. Wolfox Silverglance.

Silverglance's brother, a famous dog still found in pedigrees named Sh.
Ch. Ace of Acomb, was owned by Dr Alex Mucklow. Dr Mucklow also
owned this famous pair's sire, Sandrock Admiral. An active member of The
Weimaraner Club of Great Britain, Dr Mucklow became Vice President of
the Club in 1980. She died in 1981.

Manana Athene went on to Mrs Joan Matuszewska, to become the
foundation of the very famous Monroes affix. Mrs Matuszewska has bred
ten Champions, which is a record that still stands today. She is a lady who
knows a great deal about Weimaraners and about breeding in general. To
consistently produce Champions is no mean feat. She uses her eye, in-built

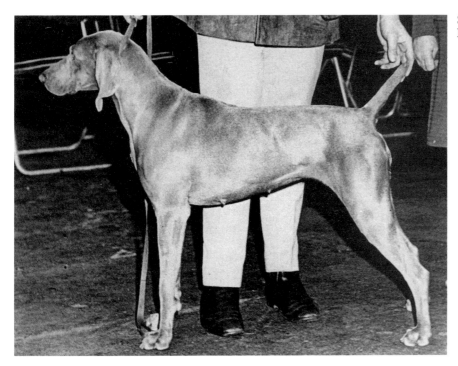

Sh. Ch. Hansom Hobby Hawk (p. 16)

instinct and great knowledge when breeding; obviously this has paid dividends.

The first Show Champion to bear her affix was Sh. Ch. Monroes Dynamic in 1963. He was the son of Athene, who was clearly a very useful brood bitch.

One dog who was very beautiful and is often found somewhere in the pedigrees of great dogs was Sh. Ch. Monroes Nexus. Monroes have headed dogs who work, show and successfully compete in Working Trials. For example, the two very successful police dogs of Paul Dodd, who were acquired from Mrs Matuszewska, bore the Monroes affix.

The Shalina affix of Tina Cutting and Sue Bradley is based on Monroes stock. Both of them breed Weimaraners capable of show and work, while preserving the Monroes affix, and when breeding like to line-breed back to the Monroes 'U' litter. I think of Monroes as being sound, 'typy' Weimaraners and many winning kennels today have a lot to thank Mrs Matuszewska for.

Kisdon's and Greyfilk

A very successful mating of Sh. Ch. Greyfilk Knightsman, winner of twelve C.C.s, and Ch. Petragua Wagtail produced three Kisdon's Sh. Ch. in Artist, who incidentally won three of his four C.C.s while still a puppy – the only Weimaraner to do this; Arabella and Asti.

Renowned for her superb movement and beautifully campaigned by her co-owner Pam Edminson, Sh. Ch. Kisdon's Asti of Nevedith ended up winning twenty-nine C.C.s in total. This has left her just two off the record for the most C.C.s. She also took three reserve (res) Groups at Championship level. She was mated with Ch. Ragstone Ryuhlan, 'Spook', winner of fifteen C.C.s, sire of three Sh. Ch. offspring and shot over by Tony Burgoin. This mating produced Sh. Ch. Kisdon's Derring-Do, winner of eight C.C.s, including one at Crufts, and the sire of nine Sh. Ch. or Ch. offspring and one New Zealand Sh. Ch. to whom he passed on his lovely colour. One of Derry's sons, Sh. Ch. Kisdon's Fagin of Sireva, won ten C.C.s and the Gundog Group in 1986 at the Bournemouth Championship Show. Most of Gill Averis' Sireva stock goes back to this dog.

Greyfilk is equally as famous an affix as Ragstone, and owners and breeders today do not have to search far back to find Greyfilk behind their good stock. Joan Fussell was a quiet, small lady of great bearing and knowledge. Her husband Ken was also involved with Weimaraners and judged the breed at Championship Show level until he died. Their daughter Nicky now shows, breeds and judges under the Greyfilk affix.

Manana Donna's Maxine, bought in 1963, was Joan's first Weimaraner, although she had been involved with other breeds before. This first bitch produced Sh. Ch. Greyfilk Sapphire, renowned by those who knew her as a beautiful specimen. The Fussells looked on her as the real foundation of the Greyfilks, always remembered for correct type and beautiful colour.

Joan Fussell developed a great friendship with Margaret Holmes, whose affix is Emmaclan. Although Margaret has not shown or bred much, she has devoted a lot of time and energy to the well-being of the breed. She was Secretary to The Weimaraner Club of Great Britain from 1971 to 1979, and then went on to become Vice President. After the death of Major R.H. Petty T.D. in April 1980, Margaret Holmes became President of the Club.

Gunalt and Hansom

Gunalt is my and my husband Stephen's affix. The foundation bitch, Vimana Viveca of Gunalt, produced Sh. Ch. Gunalt Gildoran when mated to Kisdon's Derring-Do and the winning bitch Sh. Ch. Gunalt Anais-Anais when mated to Sh. Ch. Hansom Brandyman of Gunalt, winner of nineteen C.C.s and sire of seven Sh. Ch. offspring.

Another of the Brandyman offspring, born in 1987, was Sh. Ch. Hansom Portman of Gunalt, who made breed history at two and a half by becoming the first Weimaraner to win Best in Show at Championship Show level. He

Sh. Ch. Gunalt Anais-
Anais (p. 16)

Ch. Kamsou Moonraker
von Bismarck

won BIS at the Gundog Society of Wales Championship Show, taking his
total to four Group wins and three res Group wins at Championship Show
level in addition to twenty C.C.s. His progeny have already won C.C.s and
res C.C.s; he now has two Sh. Ch. His granddam, owned and bred by Dick
Finch, Sh. Ch. Hansom Hobby Hawk, winner of thirteen C.C.s, had the
honour of becoming the first Weimaraner Championship Group Winner at
Birmingham City in 1974 and finished Best Bitch in the Show. She was the
dam of four Sh. Ch. offspring and is behind most of the great Hansoms.

Like Asti, Anais-Anais won twenty-nine C.C.s. She always did well in the
Group ring at Championship Shows and twice took the reserve place. She
won BIS at The Weimaraner Club of Great Britain Championship Show and
numerous BIS at Open Show level. One of her two Sh. Ch. offspring was
Sh. Ch. Gunalt Cacharel, who won seventeen C.C.s, was a Gundog Group
winner at Championship Show level and took two res Groups.

Other Affixes

Ch. Kamsou Moonraker von Bismarck, owned by Jane George, was
imported from the famous Kamsou Kennels in the USA in 1976. He had a
great influence on the breed as the sire of ten Champions, including one in

New Zealand, to whom he passed on his sound conformation and wonderful temperament. He won eight C.C.s and gained a show certificate in the field.

Denmo is Denise Mosey's affix and was very successful at the start of the '80s. When the foundation bitch Sh. Ch. Hansom Hirondelle was mated to Moonraker, puppies from the resulting two litters produced six Denmo Ch. or Sh. Ch. Another Denmo Sh. Ch. was by Sh. Ch. Flimmoric Fieldday.

Sh. Ch. Flimmoric Fanclub is another dog with American origins. His owner and breeder Carolyn Alston imported his dam, Luscoe's Foreign Affair of Flimmoric, from the States. His sire, Am. Ch. Nanis Totally Awesome, was bred and obtained his title in America, and spent his time in quarantine on his way to New Zealand in Great Britain, where he was mated to Foreign Affair in 1986. Fanclub gained his title and his progeny are also showing great promise, winning C.C.s and res already.

Ch. Czolkins Platinum Cirrus won a Novice Field Trial and, on winning his third C.C. he became the first Weimaraner to be qualified as a Show Champion also to win a first at a Field Trial. He won another Novice Stake and a second and third placing in a Novice Field Trial. He was the youngest winner of the Weimaraner of the Year in The Weimaraner Club of Great Britain annual competition in 1980 and is the sire of two Sh. Ch.

Sh. Ch. Kentoo Benjamin was bought as a pet by Mick and Jacqueline Ward and didn't win a First Prize until he was eighteen months old. He went on to win twenty-six C.C.s, reaching the last four in the Group at Crufts in 1985, and two res C.C.s from the Veteran Class, both at breed Championship Shows.

Sh. Ch. Ryanstock Bramble was Alison Gates' first Weimaraner. Her mother Eileen had shown Weimaraners since 1965 under the Schonblick affix. Bramble won twenty C.C.s, two Gundog Groups and three res Groups

Asta von Gut Blaustauden was imported by Mr and Mrs R. Janson. (p. 18)

at Championship Show level. Ryanstock is Kevin and Elaine Grewcock's affix. Active in the breed since 1972, both are dedicated to the Weimaraner.

Owned by Dennis White, but skilfully shown by Gerry Olsen, Sh. Ch. Trilite Tegin's Girl of Hagar has won six C.C.s, the Gundog Group at Windsor Championship Show in 1989 and res Best Gundog at Southern Counties Championship Show, also in 1989.

Other contemporary affixes to have produced Sh. Ch. or winners in the field are Absalom's Varstock, Marnie Marr's Cleimar, Mary Brennan's Amtrak, Chris and Grace Brown's Rangatira, Alison Gates' Linosa and Gill Averis' Sireva.

The Long-haired Weimaraner

This chapter cannot be complete without mentioning the long-haired Weimaraner and the introduction of longs into this country. Ann Janson instigated the popularisation of the longs and she wrote the following:

> Interest in the possibility of obtaining long-haired Weimaraners started in the late 1960s.
>
> In 1972 a long-haired bitch Pia Aus der Greifenburg was imported into England from Germany in transit to New Zealand. She was accompanied by a short-haired dog, Arno von Hohenwald, whose ancestors included long-haired dogs. They were registered with The Kennel Club but were not bred from while in the United Kingdom. They were, however, shown in an AV Gundog class.
>
> On 8 January, 1973, a litter was whelped in Scotland which contained a long-haired dog and possibly one other that died. The surviving dog puppy was subsequently registered as Mafia Man of Monroes. The remainder of this litter, bred by Mr J. Seymour, were short-haired as were the sire, Ortega Opal Mint, and the dam, Grey Moonshadow of Duenna.
>
> Later that same year a long-haired bitch, Asta von Gut Blaustauden, was imported from Austria by Mr and Mrs R. Janson, followed by a dog, Dino von der Hagardburg, in 1974.
>
> In this year too, Mafia Man of Monroes sired a litter of nine puppies out of his short-haired little sister, Uhlan Fantasia, five of which were long-haired and four short-haired.
>
> With the arrival of the bitch, Asta von Gut Blaustauden, The Weimaraner Club of Great Britain sought advice from The Kennel Club in the hope that by having a separate classification within the breed, any long-haired breeding could easily be recognisable from The Kennel Club breed register in future years. The Kennel Club decided that registration would be the same as in the country of origin, which is governed by the Fédération Cinologique Internationale, but that the coat type may be indicated on the registration certificate.
>
> 1975 saw the birth of the first all long-haired litter of eight puppies by the imports Dino von der Hagardburg and Asta von Gut Blaustauden.
>
> After long negotiations between The Weimaraner Club and The Kennel Club, the necessary amendments to the Breed Standard pertaining to the length of the coat and tail were finally approved by The Kennel Club on 2 June 1976. In all other respects the Standard was the same.

Aruni Dinwiddi from Seicer won the first C.C. for a long-haired Weimaraner. (p. 20)

Sh. Ch. Pondridge Practical Joker. This dog has been a great achiever for his owner Shirley Anderton. (p. 20)

In 1979, Mr and Mrs L. Smith imported another dog, Hasso von der Hagardburg, also from Austria. Basically breeding has centred around these four dogs with selective matings with short-haireds as advised by a geneticist of The Kennel Club team.

In spite of their small numbers several long-haireds have managed to compete favourably within the breed.

Dino von der Hagardburg, his daughter Aruni Danya from Seicer and son Aruni Dinwiddi from Seicer qualified and were shown at Crufts for the first time in 1976. The latter went on to win two C.C.s, four BOBs, over thirty First prizes at Open and Championship Shows and won a Weimaraner Club Novice Test of Work. He has qualified for Crufts every year up to 1984.

Later that same year, the bitch Aruni Danya from Seicer was the first long-haired to win Best Bitch at the Weimaraner Club Open Show. She qualified for Crufts on a further two occasions, has had many awards at Open and Championship Shows and has won a Weimaraner Novice Test of Work. Hawsvale Whitebeam won a Certificate of Merit at a novice Field Trial. Other notable winners of test of work include Monroes Fieldfare and Pondridge Aator Meragie.

When one talks of contemporary long-haireds one must think of Gill Smith's Pondridge affix. Gill and her husband Leo had their first Weimaraner in 1970, a short-haired. In 1975 the Smiths were given a puppy, Aruni Danya from Seicer, by Ann Janson. In 1979 Gill imported Hasso von der Hagardburg, from Herr Seidl of Austria and he, along with Danya and her sister Darienne, was the foundation of the Pondridge affix.

Gill's second litter by Hasso produced Pondridge Paper Moon, who is worked and has won well in the show ring at Championship Show level. She was mated to Phantom Piper of Pondridge, another dog winning well in the ring. Phantom Piper was bred by Ruth Williams and his dam Damaris Twilight has qualified CD ex, UD ex, WD ex and TD ex. His sire is Ch. Reeman Aruac, CD ex, UD ex, WD ex, and TD ex, a short-haired dog known to produce long-haired puppies. Phantom Piper was bought unseen by Gill because he comes from such sound working stock. Each Pondridge litter is monitored before breeding on, which should have the effect of producing longs very capable of competition on level terms with the short-haired Weimaraner.

Gill bred Shirley Anderton's Pondridge Practical Joker. Born on 6 September 1981, Joker has done much for long-haireds. He became the first long-haired Sh. Ch. in 1991, and has seven res C.C.s, including Crufts 1988. Certainly a dog who has aged well, after breaking a leg in 1989 and missing many of the shows, he came back out in 1990 and took a res C.C. in September of 1990. Another Pondridge, Pondridge Petronella, had five Best Puppy in Breed awards, two res C.C.s and numerous other show awards. She was also the first long-haired to be placed in the Weimaraner awards at Crufts.

2 The Breed Standard Explained

What is a Breed Standard?

Each breed of dog has to have a Breed Standard to differentiate it from other breeds. For instance, the Weimaraner is a hunting gundog and his characteristics are peculiar to him alone.

A Breed Standard is a blueprint of the perfect dog to which fanciers of that breed adhere. It is useful to all who love and want to promote the breed successfully. Therefore anyone contemplating breeding should have an in-depth knowledge of the Standard so he can try to breed the animal without exaggerating or changing the breed and losing the 'type'. It is hoped that this will have some effect in safeguarding the breed from malformations.

Showing dogs can help preserve the breed's Standard, because if a dog of, say, exceptional height or with a particularly bad temperament were exhibited he could be noted and dismissed from future breeding pro-grammes.

Of course if a breeder is 'Kennel Blind', i.e. he can see no faults in his dogs, he will not be motivated to improve their quality. Some breeders will consistently breed mediocre dogs which rarely win, because the dogs are not being bred to be improved. The breeders of these dogs invariably blame bad judging or the like for their lack of success because they don't recognise the faults in their dogs. They should take a long hard look at the Standard and interpret it correctly. Everyone should judge their dog against the Standard and be able to see his failings so that they can promote the good points when breeding on.

People interpret the Standard slightly differently and have their own personal priorities or pet likes and dislikes. For instance, one judge likes a good shoulder placement and therefore forgives a darker shade of colour because of the shoulders on the animal, whereas another judge may like a medium-sized dog and will penalise an over-sized Weimaraner.

This tends to balance out overall, because if judges read the Standard and judge accordingly, conformity to the Standard will reign supreme. The minor idiosyncrasies of the judges have the useful advantage of making you aware of different aspects of the Standard.

It is reassuring for me, when judging, to see so many Weimaraners conforming to the Standard. As a breed they are relatively sound with no major faults and long may this remain. Enthusiasts of the breed must guard the Weimaraner and discourage the 'back street breeders' that are evident in most popular breeds. They are not concerned with preserving the breed to conform to the Standard, but with the money that can be made out of breeding.

Each country has its own breed clubs and slightly differing Standards. In 1953 The Weimaraner Club of Great Britain was formed with Major Petty as its first Secretary.

Originally The Weimaraner Club of Great Britain translated the German Standard when the breed was first introduced by Major Petty. In 1987 The Kennel Club revised the Standard, making it shorter and more to the point in accordance with the parent club.

Kennel Club Standard of the Weimaraner

Characteristics

In the case of the Weimaraner, his hunting ability is the paramount concern and any fault of body or mind which detracts from this ability should be penalised. The dog should display a temperament that is fearless, friendly, protective, obedient and alert.

General Appearance

A medium-sized grey dog with light eyes, he should present a picture of great driving power, stamina, alertness and balance. Above all, the dog should indicate ability to work hard in the field. Movement should be effortless and ground-covering, and should indicate smooth co-ordination. When seen from the rear, the hind feet should be parallel with the front feet. When seen from the side, the topline should remain strong and level.

Head and Skull

Moderately long and aristocratic, with moderate stop and slight median line extending back over the forehead. Rather prominent occipital bone and ears set well back. Measurement from the top of the nose to the stop to equal that from the stop to the occipital prominence. The flews should be moderately deep, enclosing a powerful jaw. Foreface perfectly straight, delicate at the nostrils. Skin tightly drawn. Nose grey.

Eyes

Medium-sized in shades of amber or blue-grey, not protruding or too deeply set, placed far enough apart to indicate good disposition. When dilated under excitement the eyes may appear almost black. Expression keen, kind and intelligent.

Ears

Long and lobular, slightly folded and set high. The ears when drawn alongside the jaw should end approximately one inch from the point of the nose.

Mouth

Jaws strong with a perfect, regular and correct scissor bite, the upper teeth overlapping the lower teeth and set square to the jaws. Complete dentition is greatly desired. Lips and gums of pinkish flesh shade.

Neck

Clean cut and moderately long.

Forequarters

Forelegs straight and strong, with measurement from elbow to ground equalling the distance from the elbow to the top of the withers.

Body

The length of the body from the highest point of the withers to the root of the tail should equal the measurement from the highest point of the withers to the ground. The topline should be level with a slightly sloping croup. The chest should be well developed and deep, shoulders well laid and snug. Ribs well sprung, ribcage extending well back. Abdomen firmly held, moderately tucked-up flank. The brisket should drop to the elbow.

Hindquarters

Moderately angulated with well-turned stifle. The hock joint well let down and turned neither in nor out. Musculation well developed.

Feet

Firm and compact. Toes well arched, pads close and thick. Nails short and grey or amber in colour. Dew claws customarily removed.

Tail

Docked at a point such that the tail remaining shall just cover the scrotum in dogs and the vulva in bitches. The thickness of the tail should be in proportion to the body and it should be carried in a manner expressing confidence and sound temperament. In the long-haired Weirmaraner the tip of the tail may be removed.

Gait/Movement

Effortless ground covering, indicating smooth co-ordination. Seen from the rear, the hind feet should be parallel to the front feet. Seen from the side, the topline should remain strong and level.

Coat

Short, smooth and sleek. In the long-haired Weimaraner the coat should be 1 to 2 inches long on the body and somewhat longer on the neck, chest and belly. The tail and the backs of the limbs should be feathered.

Colour

Preferably silver grey; shades of mouse or roe grey are admissable. The colour usually blends to a lighter shade on the head and ears. A dark eel stripe frequently occurs along the back. The whole coat gives an appearance of metallic sheen. Small white mark permissible on the chest but not on any other part of the body. White spots that have resulted from injuries shall not be penalised. Colour of the long-haired Weimaraner as the short-haired.

Size

Height at withers: dogs 24–27 inches (61 to 69 cm), bitches 22–25 inches (56 to 64 cm).

Faults

Shyness or viciousness. Any colour or markings other than specified in this Standard. Any departure from the foregoing points should be considered a fault and the seriousness with which the fault should be regarded should be in exact proportion to its degree.

Note

Male animals should have two apparently normal testicles fully descended into the scrotum.

An Explanation of the Standard

When you read the Standard, you can see why the Weimaraner falls into a 'grey' area. Medium and moderate are words which are used to describe the dog most often. No exaggerations, highs or lows.

Characteristics

Fearless and friendly are interpreted by me to mean that this dog will stand his ground and weigh up predators, be they the wild boar or deer he was originally intended to hunt or another dog squaring up to him.

Although he is fearless, he will not start a fight or growl at other dogs for no apparent reason. It is a sign of insecurity to bite first. He should be able to recognise an insecure animal and treat it with the contempt it deserves.

The Weimaraner has the strength of character, the intelligence and power but not the aggression of some breeds of dog that combine these traits. Gundogs are bred to have soft mouths, capable of retrieving game without damaging it. This friendly nature is paramount in a gundog and applies to the Weimaraner.

If a Weimaraner is out hunting something like wild boar, which is extremely vicious and agile, and perfectly capable of turning on the hunter, he must assess the possibility of this development and be able to guard his owner. Hence we must be very aware of the protective instinct in the breed and watch for it emerging when the dog feels it is acceptable but we do not. If a Weimaraner is in the car he may feel the need to protect it. He may also feel the protective instinct take over if another dog approaches his bench at a dog show or when the dustbin men come round. He may interpret their taking of the bins as stealing and act accordingly.

His obedience must be exploited by you. A hyperactive child often has an above average intelligence that needs channelling, likewise the Weimaraner needs his intelligence exploited to bring out his obedience. His active brain and strength mean that he is alert and ready to cope with any eventuality that may arise in the field. He indicates he is physically alert when he stands erect, head high, watching all that is going on around him.

Hunting Ability   We, as custodians of this fine breed, should be concerned about preserving its wonderful hunting ability. Therefore we should not breed from stock that shows no inclination to hunt.

Not everyone wishes to shoot over their dog or to show him, but his hunting instinct can be satisfied by walks and stimulation of other kinds. Just watch him when walking on moorland or woodland. It is breathtaking to see his instinct heightened, even if you don't wish for an end result. If you love the breed make sure you can fulfil his needs before buying him.

General Appearance

The restriction on size must be adhered to. If the dog has power, stamina, and balance but is too big, we would eventually end up with a different breed. The key word is balance. This means that he does not have a shallow body and long legs, a big head and a long fine neck or strong, powerful front shoulders and weak hindquarters. Balance can be seen instantly. Each part of the anatomy is in proportion. The head, neck, length of body and hindquarters are all balanced one with the other. If the dog is too small and balanced, it may mean that he does not have enough bone and strength to provide the stamina needed for his job. If, on the other hand, he is too big and balanced, he will be 'overdone' which means exaggerated almost to the point of caricature. To carry that added bone and body during long periods of hunting and to have to stop to bend down when retrieving will require more energy and will put pressure on his joints and organs such as his heart.

Head and Skull

So much can be seen by the head. The Weimaraner has a head peculiar to himself and you should strive not to lose that look. I once heard that heads could be got back in one generation if lost, by breeding from stock with untypical heads. I don't agree; it is important to breed from good heads, because an untypical head can alter the look of the whole dog.

The Weimaraner should have a moderately long head, with a moderate stop. The stop is the raised part of the skull where the length of foreface, or nose, joins the forehead to the eyes. The length of the head and the lack of stop, in comparison with the 'prettier' breeds, is what gives the Weimaraner his snotty, aristocratic look. The skull should be broad enough to display brain room but not so wide as to be coarse. His cheeks should be full but not wide or too fleshy. This breed is a hunting breed and the Weimaraner's nose is a finely-tuned instrument. His nostrils should not be flared but must be large enough to take scent successfully.

The flews – the part of the top lips covering the jaw – should be deep enough to contain the powerful jaw but not 'snipey', which is when the lip or jowl of the dog is too short and is coupled with a long nose and narrow jaw. The flews should not be pendulous and deep; this is a clean, sleek animal and too much flew would unbalance the whole look of the head. I was told by the late Rene Goutorbe, a specialist in both show and working gundogs, that one should look for the head of a doggy bitch and a bitchy dog when choosing a puppy at eight weeks. I have applied this to Weimaraners and it is surprisingly correct. A dog with a strong head as a baby can develop a coarse head as he grows older. You should not choose a puppy with a snipey head as this will not right itself as the head alters with maturity.

The bitch with the strong head tends to 'fine down'. In a youngster the head changes and develops. If a young bitch appears to have a big head, as she grows the head will not grow at the same rate as her body and therefore will not end up as large as might have been assumed. The head will appear to be smaller in proportion to the body and, because of this different growth rate, the dog will be said to have 'fined down'. If the head continues to grow at the same rate as the body, which is more likely with a male, there is a chance of the head being coarse or overdone.

You can look at a bitch as a youngster and feel she has a very plain head, but after her first season, when her head develops, it takes on the contours of maturity and loses that stark virginal look which a lot of young bitches seem to have. In America the head of the Weimaraner seems to be finer, narrower and more snipey of muzzle than we like in Britain and with the importation of some good American stock breeders have had to be careful that we don't lose the head we prefer in getting the attributes connected with these dogs.

Eyes

The eye should be medium sized, neither bulbous nor small and piggy. If the eyes are too close together the expression will be mean and hard and the dog's sight will be impaired. If the eye is bulbous it can be lead to medical problems: the lid might not close properly, preventing proper cleansing and protection against foreign bodies that can introduce infection. There also may be problems if the haw – the loose, pendulous skin under the eye – is showing. The eye should not be tight, otherwise the dog might have difficulty closing it properly.

The expression is paramount. The Weimaraner should have that aloof, aristocratic expression which denotes his intelligence. He should not have a skitty, wild look showing the white of his eye. He should have a steady gaze.

In excitement the eyes dilate and appear almost black, but normally they will be the ghostly amber or blue-grey characteristic of the Weimaraner. At eight weeks the Weimaraner will have the most appealing piercing bright blue eyes, which over the months will lighten and take on a lovely washed-out blue colour. It is usually at about eighteen months that the eyes go amber, although this can vary. I know of a lovely Weimaraner bitch with one blue and one amber eye and I would not penalise her for this, although it is very rare.

Ears

The ears should be set high. The low set ear is usually associated with breeds that have rounder skulls. The ear is fine, long and has a distinctive fold. It should not be short or have any thickness about it. You measure the length by taking the ear along the cheek and the correct ear length will finish about an inch from the end of the nose.

A puppy's body develops at different stages, and when he is about ten weeks old his ears resemble Dumbo the Elephant's in size. It is an amusing sight to see a youngster dashing around with his great pendulous ears flapping as if he is about to take off.

Obviously the ear can be injured easily, the dog being active and the ear fine. Therefore a judge should not penalise a dog for having a bit missing from an ear or a tear in the ear.

Mouth

We often use the terms 'good mouth' or 'bad mouth' to mean teeth. A good mouth means that the dog's teeth conform to the Standard for that breed. A bad mouth is one in which the jaw is not true or teeth are missing or misplaced.

Each breed has its own priorities and some faults are regarded as worse than others. A Weimaraner is a retrieving breed so a good mouth is very important. A slightly undershot mouth or a misplaced tooth may be forgiven in some breeds but not in a Weimaraner. He should have what we call a

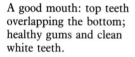

A good mouth: top teeth overlapping the bottom; healthy gums and clean white teeth.

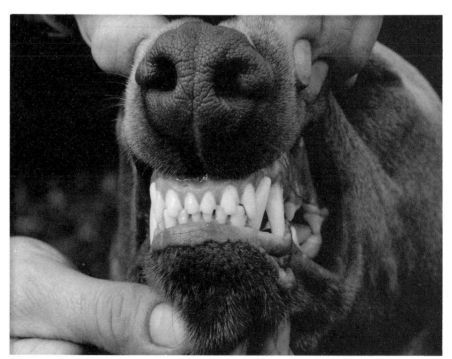

scissor bite. This means that the top teeth are slightly over the bottom teeth but remain touching. The mouth should not be overshot – the top teeth protrude over the bottom – or undershot – the bottom teeth protrude forward over the top. Sometimes an overshot mouth will right itself with time, so don't dismiss a youngster because of it. One mouth which invariably won't come right is a wry mouth, where the jaw is twisted so that the teeth are not level with each other.

These are considered faults because they could impair the dog's working ability. Also, the faults will be hereditary and if the dog is bred from, there is an increased risk of the faults being accentuated.

Complete dentition is preferred. In this country we do not pay as much attention to complete dentition as other countries do, but if dogs with incomplete dentition are bred from, this fault will be passed on and the condition worsened with time.

A Weimaraner must have a stong jaw for retrieving purposes.

Neck

A clean-cut neck means that the skin should not be overly loose or hang around the throat. 'Throatiness', as this is called, is not only unsightly but the skin also could become caught and torn. The neck should be strong enough to allow a dog to carry heavy game over walls and fences back to the gun. If the neck is too long the carrying ability is reduced; if it is too short the dog will look stocky and will have difficulty picking things up. A dog that is clean in throat or outline should not have any coarseness of bone or heaviness of body, but should be altogether refined and balanced.

Forequarters

The forequarters of the dog carry the larger part of the dog's weight, and if the shoulders are not well constructed undue pressure is put on the joints, preventing the dog from moving properly and hampering his job. If the upper arm is short the dog cannot move freely, therefore he will have to use more energy than necessary and will tire easily. This is also the case if the shoulder blade is short. The shoulder placement will be straight, impairing movement, and because the dog cannot reach forward properly the action will be 'hackneyed', which is totally incorrect. Hackneyed action is an over-exaggerated movement of the forelegs, often in conjunction with a short upper arm, that is seen as a fault because it requires extra energy. Although an exact angle is not stated in the Standard, the desired angle between the shoulder blade and upper arm is generally ninety degrees. This gives freedom of movement in front, correct reach and less stress.

The shoulder blades should not be too wide or too narrow where they meet at the withers. They will generally be too wide when the dog is upright in the shoulder. This can lead to overloaded shoulders, when the dog is over-muscled or too heavy over his shoulders. This can be caused by incorrect placement or overweight or can occur when the dog is constantly galloped over rough terrain. If the shoulder blades are too close the chest will be narrow which could cause the dog problems putting his head down. These problems can usually be seen easily by an expert and even the novice might notice something is not right, although he may not know exactly what is wrong.

If the forelegs are wide and the elbows consequently stick out, the dog is 'loose in front', and this again can be attributed to incorrect shoulders. If the dog is 'wide in front' he will invariably move badly and will often rotate his feet as he propels himself forward.

If he is too narrow in front the expression 'both legs out of the same hole' is used. The front movement is impeded and the dog will often cross his front legs when moving, giving the impression that he is 'knitting' or 'mincing', sometimes nearly tripping. If he is narrow the elbows may be nipped in and therefore the dog will turn his toes out, since it is physically impossible for him to stand correctly, and he will have to swing his legs to move.

The forelegs should be straight not bowed, the bone strong and of good quality, not fine and weak. The bone should not be coarse, especially in a dog designed for speed and endurance.

The leg is straight when viewed from the front. This is a point often muddled up by the novice judge who will write 'lovely straight front'. 'Front' here refers to the shoulder placement, but the dog should not have a straight shoulder, so obviously in that context 'lovely straight front' is a contradiction in terms. If the legs 'pin in' it means that the dog stands with straight front legs and feet turned in towards each other. The front movement would be wrong, because the legs and feet would cross, which would also impede movement.

The toes should not turn out 'east to west'. This is usually caused by weak pasterns. Weak pasterns can be a construction fault or may be caused by a lack of exercise. With correct exercise the pastern should strengthen in the latter case. A young growing dog in the process of developing can have weak pasterns and, therefore, turned-out feet; Weimaraners are not commonly 'pigeon-toed' (i.e. having turned-in feet). This will right itself in time, so don't be too worried if your juvenile has awful pasterns. As a judge I would forgive a youngster this fault. In a mature dog, I would not, as it is obviously a construction fault. When the pasterns are weak the dog will tend to flap his front feet, which is another fault.

The leg viewed from the side should be straight, showing good quality of bone in relation to the size of the dog. The dog should not be 'down on his pasterns' as this will cause him to walk on the back of his pad and he will not distribute the weight evenly. When a judge lifts the foot up and looks at the pad, he will be looking for uneven wear. This is a fault that will cause the dog to have difficulty walking in later years.

Very straight or knuckled-over pasterns – the leg slightly bows over the foot when viewed from the side – cause trouble because there is no 'give' when the dog lands on the forelegs. Therefore he will jar his body and bone structure when running or jumping. To be correct the pasterns need a very slight slope to enable them to act as a cushion or spring. Viewed from the side, the legs should tuck nicely back under the brisket – the chest, between the front legs. If you can draw an imaginary line straight from the point of the withers to the elbow the legs are in the right position.

Body

The body needs to be balanced, correctly proportioned in length, depth and width. The Standard specifies that the point of the withers to the root of the tail should equal the point of the withers to the ground. It is impractical to measure this on all dogs, but an experienced judge can tell visually if the length of the back is in the correct ratio to the height.

The withers, as with a horse, are situated at the point where the neck ends and the shoulders begin. Because height is measured at the withers, it is possible to gain or lose half an inch by the way the dog is stood. If the dog is relaxed and slouching or leaning back, he will measure less than if he is alert and quite literally 'on his toes'.

The Weimaraner should have a good length of back. Novices may assume this means he is long in loin but this is incorrect. If he is long in loin, the loin will be weak. Weakness is unacceptable and can cause him to be unbalanced.

The rib cage should extend back with the ribs evenly distributed and not cramped. The dog has thirteen pairs of ribs in all. If the shoulders are well laid back and the ribs correctly placed, the dog will be the correct length.

The chest should be well developed and deep. It should allow room for the heart and lungs to work properly and have a good 'spring of rib'. Spring of rib means that the ribs will be wide enough to allow the lungs to function and will protect the heart and internal organs from damage. The organs of an animal that is slab sided, for instance, will not be properly protected. The spring of rib should not be exaggerated, which would unbalance the dog and make him barrel ribbed. This complaint is associated with a shallow body, which does not allow enough room for the heart.

The depth in a mature animal will reach to the elbow. The depth is the measurement from the withers to the brisket. If it is too deep and/or the legs are too short, the animal will be unbalanced.

The Weimaraner should have a moderate tuck-up, which is not as pronounced as a Whippet's. The abdomen should be held firmly, giving an elegant outline to the undercarriage. Too much gut or weight on the body will lead to stress on the vertebrae and a dippy – 'sway backed' – outline. The topline should be level, flowing from the neck and sloping slightly over the croup. This does not mean that the croup should fall away with the tail set too low. If the loin is too long it will appear weak and will spoil the look of the topline. This level topline should be held while the dog is moving. If he roaches his back he will move incorrectly and his level of endurance will not be high.

The body should be well muscled over the loin, not fat, and well sprung over the ribs, not fat.

Hindquarters

This powerful, active dog needs powerful hindquarters to propel him forward and to lift him over any obstacles. If the stifle is straight it will not provide enough leverage, and if it is over-angulated, it will be weak. We sometimes see the Weimaraner in the show pose, with his hindquarters so far back that they are over-angulated. If stood correctly, just beyond the croup, the hindquarters would be higher than the forequarters and the topline would therefore be incorrect. The implications of over-angulation are that the animal is not balanced and does not have the correct proportions.

The correct bend of the stifle is similar in angle to that of the shoulder and upper arm. When a dog is working in the field scenting, with his nose to the ground, the correct bend of the stifle allows this work to proceed with minimum effort.

The tibia should be of a good length to allow the hock to be 'well let down', meaning 'lower to the ground'. This will give the hind leg better driving power.

Obviously in a breed that should work all day, you need a good degree of muscle, especially in the hindquarters. Nothing offends me more as a judge than a Weimaraner that has no muscling in the thigh and is therefore soft to the touch. The muscle should be full and lead well down. The hind leg should not go narrow just above the hock but should be filled with a good portion of muscle known as the second thigh. The lack of these muscles gives an impression of weakness. In fact, a straight stifle often goes hand in hand with poor muscling.

The main reason for lack of muscling, though, is lack of exercise and attention by the owner. This, in my opinion, is unforgiveable. People should not consider owning this particular breed unless they are willing and able to devote the time to it that it needs. Proper exercise can sometimes even help defects in the construction of the dog.

The hindquarters when viewed from the rear have the lovely rounded buttocks associated with muscle power, and wide straight back legs. However, they should not be so wide that the dog looks as if he has wet his

Good hindquarters with a correct bend of stifle. The hock is well let down, and the dog has a well-developed thigh and second thigh.

pants, nor so narrow that when he moves his legs rub together and are obviously weak. However, I quite like my 3- to 4-month-old puppy to walk a bit like he has wet his pants, which to me means he will usually end up 'right'.

The legs should be stood on squarely, with the hocks neither turned out nor in. If the hocks are turned in, 'cow hocked', it interferes with the movement of the animal. A dog with a 'good behind' has good hindquarters and is not narrow or troubled by cow hocks.

Feet

Feet are obviously very important to any creature. Without sound feet he can't walk. Nothing finishes off the look of a Weimaraner better than neat, tightly arched feet.

Flat, spread feet look unsightly and can affect the dog in a similar manner to flat feet in humans. In a coated dog flat feet are not as noticeable owing to the covering of dense hair. This is not so with the Weimaraner, though his fine coat does have the advantage of keeping his feet cleaner – he won't get snow balls or mud clogged between his toes. Also, if he becomes lame it is far easier to examine his foot for damage and to keep it clean while the injury heals.

The nails can be seen easily and therefore one needs to be extra vigilant with them. Long nails often lead to the foot spreading and make for uneven wear on the pads. The pads are the cushions of the feet and need to be thick and close to avoid sharp fragments of stone working their way between them.

Dew claws, which are the extra, small claws similar to a human thumb, are customarily removed, the Standard states. I firmly believe that because of the nature of his work, the dog is far better off having them removed. It is a simple operation performed at the same time as docking. Greater pain would be caused if a dew claw was caught in the undergrowth or was damaged as the dog jumped a wall. A wound takes considerable time to heal and bleeds profusely. Also, its position allows the dog to lick it constantly, which will delay healing. The operation, if done properly and within the first five days of life, is simple and causes no such distress.

Tail

The tail of a Weimaraner is long and thin and acts as a whip when the animal is excited. The tail should not be thick and coarse, but in balance with the rest of the animal. The tail generally suits the animal so that usually a heavy-set dog has a thick, unwieldy tail and a fine-boned animal has a thin, stick-like tail.

If the tail is docked too short, this upsets the balance of the animal. However, if it is too long, the tail has a tendency to wave about and to look untidy. It should be carried in such a manner as to express confidence and sound temperament.

It has been said that a Weimaraner carrying his tail straight up or over his back is expressing confidence. This simply isn't true. A tail carried in such a way is a sign of aggression or, at the very least, a sign that the dog is on the defensive, with his senses heightened. A tail carried in confidence is at an angle and denotes the bearer's friendly, fearless temperament.

Another bad fault in a tail is if it appears to be glued down. The dog is expressing an insecure or nervous temperament – a 'bite first and ask questions later' attitude. The tail tells us a lot about the animal as a whole, and is an important part of the anatomy.

Gait/Movement

If the dog is made right, he will invariably move right. As explained earlier in this chapter, if he is upright in the shoulder he will not have front extension. If he is weak in the hindquarters, he will move 'close behind' – the hind legs almost touch as he moves away from you at a trot. When viewed from the rear the dog's legs should move straight back, parallel with the front legs. The dog is said to be 'crabbing' when he twists in the back and the back legs move diagonally to the front legs. They should not be close, crossing or too wide. The gait should be effortless and free moving, and from the side the topline should remain level, with the dog driving on or pushing off from the hocks. A dog 'moves like a train' when each properly constructed part flows with the next, and if he moves in this manner you can generally say with confidence that he is 'as sound as a bell'.

Many judges judge the animal on movement alone, but this has to be wrong. A Weimaraner is a distinctive breed and is made in a way peculiar to him. Movement should be taken into account with 'type'. I once had a dog who moved straight and true, with drive. To me he lacked 'type', but it didn't stop him winning. Another dog tended to throw his off fore foot when moving. He had 'type' and quality and went on to produce some fine stock. Out of the two he would be the one I would want over the other.

The Weimaraner is an ungainly walker because of his construction. He is not intended to excel at walking. When judges ask me to walk a Weimaraner for them in the ring, I get the feeling that they do not fully understand the breed. A clever handler will move his dog at home in front of a friend. Thus he will be able to ascertain the best speed to move his dog to promote his good points. This is not dishonest or intended to hide any faults, because a good judge who knows his job will be able to detect them.

Coat

This is fairly self-explanatory. If the animal is in good condition, mentally as well as physically, due to good food and exercise, he will have a healthy bloom on his coat. If he is neglected in any way his coat will be dull and lifeless. This applies to both the short- and long-haired varieties.

A short-coated Weimaraner should not have long hair nor should the coat appear thick or wavy. It should be short, close, smooth and sleek.

Colour

The very beautiful *true* silver grey is a sight to behold, but shades of mouse or roe grey are also permitted. Very often the term pale is applied to the colour of the coat. This means that the animal could be sandy coloured as opposed to grey. This is just as much a fault as a darker colour.

The silver-grey colour is unique to the Weimaraner, as is his wonderful physique. Even if he were seen only in silhouette he would be recognisable and we must bear these factors in mind when reproducing this breed. However, if we breed for colour only, we run the risk of losing type.

For me the colour is most apparent when watching the Weimaraner quartering on a grouse moor. He is easily distinguished from all other dogs by his ghostly, irridescent colour. I often wonder if Sir Arthur Conan Doyle had such a sight in mind when he penned *The Hound of the Baskervilles*.

White is acceptable only in a small white patch on the chest. Breeders with far more experience than I say that to preserve the unique silver grey one must expect a touch of white to come through on occasion, probably more than is acceptable in the ring. However, I have seen some super dogs achieve the title of Show Champion with white in other places than the chest or with a larger than preferred amount of white on the chest.

We must keep this in perspective. If the attributes of the animal outweigh the disadvantage of a flash of white behind the pastern or on the undercarriage then he should win, because this fault has been weighed up against the faults of his competitors in the class and deemed the lesser.

White may well be evident on a young puppy when you purchase it. If the degree of white is high and you wish to show it, don't buy it. A caring, reputable breeder will not try to foist such a puppy on somebody wishing to show, but this whiteness will not make a less loving or loyal pet.

A youngster will often develop a darker donkey stripe along the length of his back. This is nothing to worry about and usually grows out successfully.

Your Weimaraner may moult. Bitches moult more frequently than dogs, especially after a season. Often during her season her coat will appear patchy or woolly, with a touch of ginger. A coat in moult may take on the appearance of having spots rather like rain drops. When the dog is through the moult, the coat will revert to its normal condition. The new coat may appear darker initially. However, this soon alters and may eventually end up even lighter than the original coat.

Regular grooming during the moult helps. If the coat is in really bad condition, I find that a little cooking oil massaged into the coat and skin can help.

The coat often lightens with age. I believe that the dog's environment also plays a part: whether the dog lives in a house or a kennel affects the colour. Some foods appear to affect the colour, although this is theory, not fact.

Size

Height variations can be quite extreme. A judge has to be careful not to penalise an animal that is within the permissible size range. Although a well-balanced animal in the middle of the range is preferred, an animal on the periphery is acceptable.

However, we must remember that to breed from an animal at an extreme of the Standard will eventually alter the breed. If you breed from stock in the middle of the range, then you have the option of producing taller, shorter or the same size offspring. But if you consistently breed from an oversized dog, then you will consistently produce a higher percentage of taller puppies; likewise with small animals. If that trend continues, then breeders will wish to alter the Standard. The Standard height was chosen as the most effective height for the Weimaraner's particular function. A smaller dog will generally not have the stamina for a full day's work. A taller dog will have to use more energy to lower himself to scent, work and retrieve and will tire unduly. Therefore, the Standard should be adhered to when breeding.

It may look impressive to have a dog standing 28 or 29 inches tall, but it is most definitely wrong. We all produce the odd one out of the Standard, but it should be the exception not the rule. We must also think very carefully about showing or breeding it.

Quality

The one thing a dog needs, which is not listed in the Standard and which can only be seen and not defined, is quality. Quality in conjunction with balance and a distinguished style are what sets one dog apart from the rest. There are many good dogs, but only a few great ones that have all of these attributes. I often think of a bitch that I used to watch being shown. Parts of her could have been improved, but when judged as a whole she had all three attributes in plenty and so was unbeatable.

3 Buying and Feeding a Weimaraner

Deciding to Buy a Weimaraner

A lot of ground work has to be done before you actually buy your puppy. Don't rush out and buy a puppy that is advertised in the local paper, just because the breed is currently in fashion. Remember that once you buy a puppy he becomes your responsibility, so make sure your reasons for wanting a Weimaraner are good ones. Before you rush out to buy the first Weimaraner you come across, do some very serious research into the breed, and any other breed you may think is suitable for your household and circumstances.

A Weimaraner is large, athletic, powerful and needs plenty of time and exercise. If you are employed full time or live in a town in a house with hardly any garden a Weimaraner is perhaps not the dog for you. Maybe a cat would be more suitable: they are much more independent and are happy to be left alone for long periods of time and exercise themselves.

Weimaraners and Children

People ring me to ask if a Weimaraner is good with children. This is a logical question, as most people think about buying a dog when the wife has left work to have children, or when the children have started school, and the wife has some free time to devote to the puppy to train and rear him well. In those conditions, yes, a Weimaraner gets on well with children. If, on the other hand, the people ringing want a Weimaraner to amuse and occupy the children while they do something else, the answer is no.

Weimaraners are mentally strong dogs and will become wilful and disobedient if not reared with authority and determination. A young child does not have that authority and therefore you will end up with a badly behaved dog. Weimaraners find children vaguely boring because they do not mentally stimulate them and so lose interest in them quickly. After a while in a child's company a Weimaraner will usually go off on his own, doubling the original problem, not alleviating it.

If you are looking for a dog specifically for the children, think about a Cocker Spaniel or some other breed that is very friendly, small enough for a child to handle competently and enjoys being in the company of children for long periods of time. Having said that, do not contemplate buying a dog that children will abuse, as this will end in disaster for all concerned.

A dog is an ideal way to teach children respect for others, human or canine. Dog ownership also teaches children the art of sharing and helps them to understand that we all have to do things we don't want to do, for whatever reason.

Obviously children cannot be taught the same black and white rules that you teach puppies. They do things on impulse, which is why we need to teach puppies that humans of any age are higher in the pecking order than themselves and are allowed to do things that puppies are not. Children, on the other hand, should be taught that they can play with the new puppy, but they must respect him and not treat him roughly.

Children have a natural desire to pull at a puppy's front legs and tail. They should always be stopped from doing this. I must stress that no one should pull a dog's legs nor should he ever pull the front legs apart in a split position. The puppy's heart is suspended in the chest cavity and pulling the front legs apart can tear the heart, killing the dog.

Mistreatment can turn an amenable, loving pup into one with an aggressive nature. Only let children play with the pup, or indeed an adult dog, under adult supervision.

Use as a Guard Dog

I would not sell a Weimaraner as a guard dog. People who want guard dogs often want big dogs that look vicious, which they can goad into becoming mean and aggressive. They are not suitable owners of Weimaraners or of any dog.

A Weimaraner has a soft mouth. He is not designed to kill, but is the hardest of all gundogs. Having said that, a Weimaraner is very protective of his own, and would be capable and willing to protect his owners against attack if necessary, which is a nice feeling to have about a dog.

Environment

People who live in the country think that they live in the ideal conditions for owning a Weimaraner. This is true if the dog is kept properly; if not, they can be the worst conditions.

The Weimaraner's instincts are very strongly bred into the dog. Hence if you think that because your house backs onto a farm, moorland or other open area that a Weimaraner is ideal for you and you let the dog roam free, you are asking for very serious trouble.

It is very easy to get into the habit of opening the door and letting the dog have a free run over the hills and vales. Once you start letting a youngster have his head in such a way it is difficult to stop him, and you will end up having him shot by an angry farmer when he grows up and continues to trail.

Consequently, as strange as it may seem, it can be kinder to buy a Weimaraner if you live in a town. It all depends on your animal husbandry. If your conditions are restricted, you have to make an effort to walk the dog. There is no alternative.

You must be prepared to get up in foul, damp, foggy, windy conditions at the crack of dawn to take the dog for a walk before the real work of the day begins. Or had you conjured up idyllic sunny summer morns or glorious autumn mornings with crisp, bright leaves underfoot? We don't often have clean, white, virgin snow, but we do have cold, wet slush, that cars splash over you as they drive past. Maybe now is the time to consider a small breed that does not need all this exercise; but then you would miss the devotion and love of a Weimaraner, or the wonderful feeling that you get as you watch a Weimaraner galloping across the moors, every instinct heightened, almost irridescent and ghostly, making it easy to see how the Grey Ghost got his name.

Your Future

When thinking of buying a large, mentally strong breed, remember that he will probably live to the age of eleven or twelve. The decision that you make now is going to affect your life for some considerable time. For instance, if you decide to emigrate you might have to find another home for your dog, or your wife might decide to return to work once the children have grown up. It isn't fair to keep the dog locked up all day, but is it fair to expect him to change home and family? Desertion is the same for a dog as it is for a child. Try to envisage your long term future and lifestyle before you buy a puppy. You could end up causing him a lot of heartache if you don't.

I remember a couple coming to see us about Weimaraners. They came back again after the initial visit, having discussed the advantages and disadvantages and decided that the Weimaraner was the right dog for them. On the subsequent visit we discussed what the alternatives would be if the wife decided to return to work at a later date. We discussed one possibility, the outside kennel and run. This had to be bought and set up initially to allow the pup to become used to it, without stress to him or his owners. The puppy would be confined to it for a short period each day, which would do him no harm and would allow him to become accustomed to it, knowing that in a little while he would be back with the family. This way he would be happy in it and it would be *his* kennel.

Puppies sleep a lot and the kennel is a good place for a puppy to rest without disturbance and distractions. If at some future date the woman returns to work, the Weimaraner will be able to stay in his kennel and run without stress and confusion, knowing that she is out but that she will come back. He is confined but he has the freedom to potter about outside should he so wish, and mum has peace of mind.

When we sell a puppy to people such as those I have just described, I feel confident that the puppy is going to the right environment. The family did not rush their decision, but weighed up all the factors before making their final decision.

Your Ability to Rear the Puppy

Sometimes people who have owned dogs before are confident that having reared a puppy once they will have no problems doing it again with a Weimaraner puppy. However, having a much loved dog for ten or so years and then purchasing a puppy expecting him to be exactly the same can be a shock. Don't try to compare them. Bear in mind that an eight-week-old puppy can never be similar to an old dog and is always going to be ten times the work. It is hard work, but done properly and with consideration it is well worth doing.

Your Age

Your age must also be considered when you are thinking about buying a dog. An older couple came to us wanting a Weimaraner, but I felt extremely apprehensive as to their suitability. They assured me that they would be able to manage this big gundog beautifully, as they had only recently lost their thirteen-year-old Rottweiler bitch. A Rottweiler is a big, strong guard dog, but by no means as active, physically or mentally, as a Weimaraner. It is as different to deal with as a Jack Russell Terrier is to an Afghan Hound!

The difference between owning a pup when you are forty-six years old and when you are fifty-nine, when you aren't as fit or as able, has to be considered carefully. Would this couple be able to cope with the same breed thirteen years on, never mind one that they weren't used to that has far more energy? I advised them against buying a Weimaraner.

Costs

Another point to consider before buying a pup is whether you can afford him for the duration of his life. When people ring me enquiring about Weimaraners and their first question is 'How much are they?' I am filled with trepidation. The initial cost of the pup is not the final figure nor is it what owning a Weimaraner is all about. You have to consider the costs throughout his life, i.e. price, habitat, food, medical expenses, boarding kennel fees – the list is endless.

Even if your dog never ails in his life, he still has to be inoculated and wormed regularly. He is an active, brave hunting dog and is therefore prone to cuts and injury. These, if serious, can be very expensive, especially with visits to the vet for stitches and treatment.

Boarding kennel fees also have to be considered as part of your long-term expenditure, as you will no doubt be going on holiday at some point and you cannot leave him at home unattended.

Food is, of course, the most regular expense that you will incur. Weimaraners are not cheap to run, but there is no need to be excessive. You may also find it necessary to change your car to a bigger model. A puppy can be as expensive as a new baby!

Where to Buy Your Puppy

Once you have decided you want a dog and the dog is to be a Weimaraner, ring as many dog agencies as you can, i.e. The Kennel Club or dog publications such as *Dog World* or *Our Dogs*, for a list of reputable breeders. Word does get around and if someone has a bad reputation, often agencies know and won't recommend him, but they are very happy to recommend a breeder with a good name. Always go to a breeder, never to a pet shop or a dealer.

At a pet shop or dealer's you only see the puppy. This gives you no indication of what it will be like as an adult. Also, you will not see the mother. It is important that you do, because it will give you an idea of her temperament, size and fitness, and you will be able to see for yourself if she has any glaring hereditary faults. Most importantly, if you buy from a dealer or pet shop you will not receive any after-sale support with your puppy. They usually do not know the dog or breed intimately enough to be able to offer you any worthwhile advice.

Dealers usually acquire their puppies from ignorant breeders who can't sell them, and who are ignorant in the sense that they put their bitch to the nearest dog available, without giving any thought to the implications of their actions in terms of line breeding or doubling up on poor genes. Other people do know the consequences and breed pups purely to sell to dealers. They don't care about the pups they breed and are only doing it for the money. Either way, you generally will not get a carefully planned, well-bred puppy from anyone but a reputable breeder.

Make an appointment to go and see two or three breeders. You will be able to listen to what they all have to say and will get an idea about what their priorities are when breeding a litter and how much confidence you have in what they are saying. If you visit and talk to a breeder, you will learn so much that you won't have access to anywhere else. You will also get some idea of what owning such a dog will let you in for.

Every breeder has a different image of the perfect Weimaraner. Beauty is in the eye of the beholder. Only by visiting a breeding establishment can you marry what you want with what a particular breeder wants.

It may be best to visit before the breeder has a litter for sale. That way you can look and listen objectively and make up your mind, without being swayed by adorable puppies with neon signs in their eyes saying, 'Buy me, I'm for sale'. The breeder will also be able to assess your needs without subconsciously thinking, 'I have to find a home for this male puppy I have left'. That way you won't end up with an unsuitable puppy, which would lead to dissatisfaction and unhappiness all round.

A litter should be carefully bred and, therefore, there should be no discrepancy in the price of the puppies. If more is charged for bitches, it implies that they are worth more because of their breeding potential. This should not be the case.

You must have confidence in your breeder, because you may need his support to enjoy your puppy fully. If you encounter various trivial problems and can't decide how best to deal with them, you should be able to ring your breeder for advice. He will want to help make the problems disappear before they become full-blown traumas, and you can learn from his experience.

When you have finally decided which breeder you will buy your puppy from, it is a good idea to leave your name, address and telephone number so that he can contact you when a litter is born. On the other hand, you may find it easier to take the breeder's name and number, find out when the next litter is due and give him a ring at that time. Don't leave it until the puppies are old enough to go to their new home, as you will probably find that by then they will all be spoken for and you will not have time to organise your home for the new arrival.

We always let people come and see the puppies whenever they want, within reason. The pups are striped two shades of grey for the first few days of their lives and potential new owners find this fascinating and adorable. They also like to have photographs of the pup for the family album as quickly as possible. We often have prospective owners visiting the pups weekly to record their development.

It is time-consuming and, in all fairness, can be something of a nuisance for the breeder, but with thought on both sides visits can be rewarding for all concerned. It is important for the new owner to form a bond with the pup if they so desire. However, some breeders prefer that the owners do not see the pups for the first couple of weeks, feeling that it disturbs the bitch and puppies and also carries the risk of introducing disease to the kennel. These

Weimaraner puppies are fascinating at four weeks of age, whether long-haired or short-haired. The difference is seen easily.

are valid concerns and it is up to the breeder to determine his own rules.

Rescue

Sometimes genuine, well-behaved, faultless Weimaraners end up in rescue and one feels very sorry for all concerned. However, the most common reason for a dog needing rescue is human error in purchasing or training the dog, or neglect.

Most caring breeders will willingly take back dogs they have bred. This is very good as not only does it relieve the pressure on the hard-worked rescue service run by The Weimaraner Club of Great Britain, but also the breeder should know the temperament of dogs he breeds and he will, if anyone can, be able to instill in the dog new and good habits after the initial problems are sorted out. Dogs without papers or pedigrees are more of a problem, because you have no way of knowing their genetic traits.

Owners who are riddled with guilt are often too shame-faced to go back to the breeder for help and use the rescue service as a way out. If you ever feel the need to part with your Weimaraner have the courage, for his sake, to go back to the breeder and give that dog the best possible chance.

Every person connected with re-homing dogs, through whatever medium, has his own opinions and feelings about what is required of the family wishing to take an older dog with any minor or major problems. The one thing generally agreed upon is that you need to have your eyes wide open when taking on such a dog.

Some people think it will be easier taking on an older dog than a puppy, but it isn't. A puppy learns quickly and if you are wise, he learns your habits from the moment you acquire him. An older dog has different standards and routines from you and your family ingrained in him.

You can keep a puppy in an indoor kennel so that he doesn't chew, but an older dog will not be so amenable or willing to be caged and might try to destroy it. He might never have been left before and will bark and howl whenever you turn your back – a difficult habit to break in an older dog. Likewise you and he might have different ideas about where he should sleep, and he might take exception and bear his teeth.

If he had always been yours you should be confident enough in his behaviour to exert your supremacy. However, if you have had his attributes and faults relayed to you by the previous owner, who is to say they are accurate? No one likes to admit they have failed, so they might have forgotten to mention some of the worst offences.

When taking on an older dog, you will need a completely open mind and not expect anything from him. It is a rare and caring person that can care for dogs with such special problems. Some feel that they will be able to change the dog, but this is the wrong attitude when dealing with an older dog. You need to re-educate him, which takes patience and knowledge. You will need to be firm but kind. Hard and fast rules do not always work with a rescue. You will need to be flexible and learn to read the dog, because he is capable of acting out of character over a long period of time, not just within the first fortnight.

Some people like the idea of having a rescue because it is much cheaper than buying a puppy. Not only is this totally unacceptable ethically, but it is also untrue. He will probably have cost you a lot more by the time you have ironed out all his problems.

Before the Weimaraner is re-homed, his history has to be carefully studied. His character needs to be assessed by somebody with years of experience in the breed. If there is the slightest doubt about his temperament, then he must never be re-homed in a family with children.

You have to be able to read the dog and the situation. You cannot get it right all of the time. It is a hard, thankless task, taking on a rescue, but if you do and it is successful, the rewards you reap will be tremendous.

How to Choose Your Puppy

People often say, on hearing that the litter has been born, 'When can I come and choose my pup?'. Maybe they think that if they don't have first choice, they will get an inferior puppy. However, I defy anyone to choose a Weimaraner puppy from, say, a litter of eight at two days or even two weeks old. In fact, you can ask someone to choose a pup at eight weeks and five minutes later they won't be able to tell you which one it was. It may be better to let the breeder advise you as to which one he thinks will suit your needs best.

The character of a puppy starts to develop at about four weeks and as the breeder feeds and watches the litter, he learns which one is a hooligan, which is refined and which is a loveable rogue. Therefore he is able to match puppies to owners better than someone who only sees them for a short period of time.

I remember one litter we had where we matched pups to owners. A lady, strong in character, wanted a pup to rear as a pet. She didn't work and had a lot of time and energy to devote to the pup, as well as a large country garden. One puppy in the litter was very bright and very active. The lady took that puppy and has the most wonderful pet to this day, because the strong character of the lady complemented the strong character of the pup.

Another puppy in the litter, a dog, was very quiet and almost withdrawn, but neither shy nor nervous. The other puppies, the bitches in particular, bullied him. Although he was the largest puppy, he would sit in the corner and look worried at his treatment by his litter mates. The lady we thought would suit him was of a sensitive disposition. She developed his character with her gentle ways and has ended up with a gentleman of a dog who worships the ground she walks on.

If the puppies had gone to the opposite owners, they would have ended up with the outgoing pup running rings round the sensitive lady and the quiet puppy's character being broken by the dominant owner. This provides a good case in point for letting your breeder choose a puppy for you. The breeder will not demand that you take a certain puppy or none, but will guide your decision for the good of all.

Some people say that you shouldn't choose the pup that sits in the corner but the lively, confident one. Maybe they assume that the lively one is the most intelligent and the fittest, whereas the quiet one isn't. Weimaraners are very intelligent dogs and I find that the quiet pup is often very bright and deep thinking – if it is bred soundly – and is therefore a good choice. The lively one can often have a very instinctive working spirit, which may not suit the average family who wants the puppy purely as a pet.

If you have researched your breeder well and have confidence in him, the puppies will be fit but if they are not this will be pointed out and explained. A good breeder will not try to hide anything.

Double Trouble

'I want two puppies' is a statement I dread. Two puppies are not double happiness, they are double *trouble*. People think two will keep each other company, play together and stop each other from becoming lonely. This is true to a certain extent, but it also eases the owner's guilt about leaving one puppy alone. Has that owner not thought that if he cannot do justice to one puppy he will be dividing what little attention he can give by two?

Don't feel guilty, because one puppy will soon settle down and be happy if you do your job properly. When you have one small puppy you have the time and enthusiasm to devote to him properly. You can watch him like a hawk and housetrain him quickly. With two puppies it becomes more complicated: for instance, which one do you take out to go to the toilet and which do you scold when there has been an accident?

Lead training can be tedious with one puppy but it is practically impossible with two. A puppy needs taking out and talking to all the time. He needs to be restrained constantly and to be shown the way you require him to walk. Will you always have time to take the two of them for walks separately?

Doing things with puppies individually is important, which defeats the purpose of having two at the same time. When you leave one of them on his own, he will become jealous because the other pup is receiving more attention. I'm not saying that you would encounter these problems with other breeds of dog, but Weimaraners are very possessive and jealous of any other dog getting attention. They also need play training from the moment you have them and don't share that learning process easily.

Another point is that the two puppies will reach old age together. If they are from the same litter they stand a chance of dying of the same complaint and doubling the heartache when they come to the end of their natural lives.

Two Weimaraners are wonderful, but they shouldn't be the same age. Get A to 18 months or more and out of his juvenile problems before thinking about B. A will then help to rear B and will be an example to him, and together they will give you immense pleasure. Our older and wiser dogs rear our puppies very successfully these days and teach the babies good manners.

If you wish to keep two dogs, should they be of the same sex, or one of each? The problems arise when the bitch comes in season, as it is not possible to keep them in the same environment. The answer is either to have one neutered or accept the fact that every six months you are going to have to board the bitch.

If you have two dogs it is probably wise not to use either or both of the dogs for stud purposes, especially if they are house pets. This would be the fastest way to upset the equilibrium. The worst thing you can do to two males living together is to create a barrier between them. If you separate them, re-introduce them carefully. Even separating them to show one and not the other can cause petty jealousies. If growling occurs on the re-introduction, give them a chew each to distract them and tell them not to be silly.

Worrying and keeping them apart only makes matter worse, causing more bad feeling and making it even harder to settle them back together. If the worst really does happen, take them to neutral ground, where neither has the mental upper hand, before letting them become friends again. If your dogs are sensibly bred and trained and see you as the pack leader you should not have major problems.

Two bitches usually get on well together, so long as you remember that they may suffer from hormonal changes which could affect their temperament. A bitch in season might well fight with a bitch that she is normally best friends with. Remember, bitches fighting can be as dramatic and dangerous as dogs. If the situation looks like it is getting out of hand, a stern word and a riding crop usually have the desired effect (see Chapter 4).

If a serious fight does occur, never rush in to separate them. You will only succeed in getting badly hurt yourself. Find a hose or bucket of water or even a twangy stick and wade in with that. Never intervene unarmed, or you may be 'unarmed'.

Bringing Your Puppy Home

The day dawns when you are due to pick up your new puppy from the breeder and bring him home. The best time for this is in the morning. It won't hurt him to be picked up in the afternoon or early evening, but morning is best for him and you. This is because you will have the rest of the day to familiarise him with his new friends and environment.

When you pick your new baby up from the breeder, you should take with you a towel and roll of kitchen paper. You can also take a blanket, a large cardboard box, some chews, a collar, newspaper and perhaps a little drink of milk, but I would say all you will really need is a towel in case he dribbles or drools and kitchen paper in case something needs cleaning up on the way. The rest can wait until he gets home.

If he were a new baby and not a puppy, you would give him and yourself a few days to settle before you began showing him off to friends and relatives. Try to give your puppy the same consideration. Remember his circumstances have changed completely and he needs stability and continuity until he is secure in his new surroundings. If you deal sympathetically with the situation, your relationship with him will be on a sound footing straight away.

Bringing a puppy home at Christmas time can pose special problems. If you have researched your breed and have planned ahead, you might decide, because of the long holiday at Christmas, that you would like to pick up your puppy on Christmas Eve or even Christmas Day. This is the worst thing you could do. However, the idea of getting a puppy when there is a holiday is good. Arrange to pick the puppy up the day after Boxing Day, when everything has returned to normal, presents have been put away, over-eating, drinking and socialising have settled down and the puppy can come to a more normal household.

When you pick up your puppy, you will be provided with a diet sheet, pedigree and registration forms and a list of do's and don'ts. Your puppy should have been wormed at least twice, depending on his age. We worm puppies at four, six and eight weeks of age.

All dogs have worms, but these are kept under control by regular worming, making the worm lie dormant in the dog's intestinal tract. When a bitch is in whelp, hormones activate the worms; therefore, all puppies are born with worms. It is best to buy your worming preparation from your vet and to seek his advice on treatment. You can then be sure that it will be safe and effective for your puppy.

Try to stick to the diet sheet provided initially. This will help settle your puppy in his new home, because the less change he has to undergo, the less stress he will suffer.

When your puppy arrives in his new home, let him potter about at will, sniffing and weighing up his new surroundings. Offer him a small drink of water, but no food immediately, especially if he has travelled badly. Don't crowd him or let the children pester him. Give him time and space to accustom himself to you all. Remember that he needs to sleep and this is important as he uses this time to grow strong and healthy.

Children should always be taught to respect animals and your puppy will help with this. They must realise that a puppy is not an animated stuffed toy, but a living baby that needs to be treated as such. Likewise the puppy must learn respect for them. He should not be allowed to bite in play as he would with his brothers and sisters, nor should he play inside the house with too much exuberance or roughness. He will not understand if you let him get away with it when he is young and then change the rules when he becomes a problem.

Your dog is required by law to wear a collar with a name tag. This is in case he is lost or found injured. After a week or so, when your puppy has settled in, put a soft collar on him for a short period each day. Gradually leave the collar on for longer periods until he can wear it all day. As he grows, check and change the collar to fit; don't indulge in an expensive collar until he is fully grown.

The Vet

Make an appointment to see your vet. This is for two good reasons. First, you will be able to meet your vet and establish a good relationship with him before he is required in a serious capacity and, if by any chance you don't like him, it gives you time to find one you do like before you need him. I feel very strongly that you should have a good relationship with your vet, because then you won't worry about his reaction if you have to ring him in the dead of night or if you want reassurance about your dog, and you will feel confident in his treatment of your dog. Secondly, you will need him to give your pup a medical. A good breeder does not like to sell an unhealthy pup, so this check is for you, your puppy and the breeder. At the same time the vet will advise you on the course of inoculations your puppy will require and when.

Vets and breeders should work together, accepting the role each plays. Nothing is achieved if the breeder is anti-vet and tries to do the vet's job, or vice versa. It is the vet's job to advise about the future health care of the pup. The vet knows the area the pup will live in and can advise appropriate care for him.

If you tell him that your breeder asked you to come to him for advice on inoculations, worming, etc., it will establish an immediate rapport with him and he will do his best for you willingly. Having said all that, don't feel intimidated by your vet. People have told me horrific tales of vets snapping at them for ringing out of hours. Courtesy, civility and consideration is your due as well as his, and are the keys to a long and successful relationship.

Vets are very expensive, as they run private practices. It may well be worth considering an insurance scheme to cover your dog for vet fees, death, etc. Although Weimaraners tend to be a very healthy breed, they do have lots of vitality and enthusiasm, and this, coupled with a fine coat, makes them prone to cuts and other injuries. Obviously a Weimaraner is an expensive animal to buy and although money will not replace a much loved companion, it is sensible to consider his insurance in the cold light of day, before something drastic and unforeseen happens. Veterinary surgeries usually have leaflets from several animal insurance companies and no doubt your vet will have had clients who swear by one company and not another. You might even be able to ask the breeder to take out a temporary cover for you and then have the company send you details of a year's cover.

Nails

The breeder will have cut the puppy's nails several times. It is a good idea to keep to this practice. There is nothing more ugly, or uncomfortable for the dog than long talons, which make his feet spread and create difficulty in walking. If you cut the nails regularly when he is a pup, it slows down the growth process as an adult. The bathroom clippers will be adequate for a youngster, but as the nails harden you will need to purchase canine clippers.

Of course there is always the argument put forward by breeders and vets that your dog will wear his nails down naturally when walking on the road or any hard surface. In my experience he will not. My husband and I have had

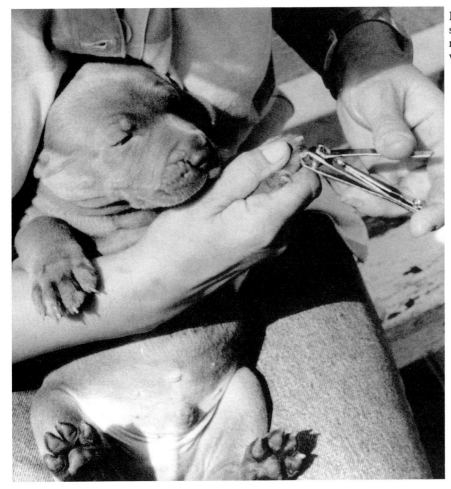

It is wise to keep the nails short. Start by cutting the nails when the puppy is very young.

numerous dogs: some wear them down and some do not. Don't assume that you will be lucky, because if you are not and you have not got him used to having his nails cut, you will find it difficult to restrain him and the quick of the nail will be long, so that the nail cannot be reduced successfully.

Food and Feeding

Everyone has their own ideas and staunchly defends their ways of feeding. The trouble is everyone you encounter when you get a new puppy, and throughout his life, will want you to feed your dog according to their feeding regime. The best solution is to listen, take in what they say and see what works for your dog.

Weimaraners are sensitive to change, be it in food or your mood, so you can upset them by worrying about their feed, consequently forming a vicious circle.

In his wild state the dog is an omnivore rather than a carnivore. He needs a certain amount of vegetable matter as well as meat for a balanced diet. Before the convenience of dog foods that we have today, dogs would be fed scraps and fat not eaten by humans, and lights or lung, with stale bread, crude biscuit, flaked maize and any mixture of cereal to add bulk, without real thought or knowledge of the dog's needs in terms of vitamins and minerals, proteins, carbohydrates or fats. Clever breeders and dog men got it right by instinct, balancing the ingredients. Others got it hopelessly wrong, and dogs suffered all sorts of disorders and their life was shortened as a result. The pet food industry is a big business today and manufacturers spend vast amounts of money perfecting the balance of nutrients within their particular brands to keep our dogs in top condition, gleaming with good health throughout their lives.

Every living thing needs feeding to continue life. Dogs basically need food to maintain a healthy life, and a good sensible diet provides a normal dog with energy to grow, reproduce and carry on normal bodily functions, and fuel to keep moving and fight off disease.

The energy the normal dog needs is gained from proteins and carbohydrates and can be converted to fat to be stored in the body. If this is not watched, however, obesity will result. Some breeds are more prone to obesity than others. The Weimaraner, due to his mental and physical formation, is not among these breeds, but he should not be over-indulged.

A normal dog requires a diet consisting of about twenty per cent protein which helps provide body-building materials and mental stimulation. Milk, for the young, meat of all kinds, fish and eggs, all provide our dogs with proteins. For the vegetarian-minded soya, beans and pulses also help provide proteins, although I feel a dog, especially a Weimaraner, should have the opportunity to eat meat and not be subjected too strongly to our social beliefs.

Fats are needed for a healthy diet. These provide energy and warmth and keep the skin and coat in good condition. We found that adding a teaspoon full of wheatgerm oil to our Spaniel's food noticeably improved his condition and cleared his skin trouble.

Vitamins and Minerals

The need for vitamins and minerals is recognised in a well-balanced diet. Additives must be used cautiously because they can prove detrimental in some cases. For instance too much calcium in youngsters was thought to cause the incorrect growth of the jaw leading to a malformation of the teeth placement or 'bite'.

Vitamins A and D are found in milk, cream and animal fats. Vitamin A can also be found in green vegetables. Vitamin A helps keep the dog healthy and fight infections. Vitamin D is needed to utilise the calcium and phosphorus. Dogs interestingly have no need for Vitamin C except in extreme cases. Vitamin B is found in meat, liver, milk and eggs but is killed by eating egg white raw and through cooking. This vitamin is also found in yeast.

Dogs that eat their own excrement are likely to be deficient in Vitamin B and giving yeast tablets will stop this dreadful habit. I find bitches are more likely to eat excrement than males and this could be instinctive, since bitches clean up after their puppies for the first three or four weeks of life. I also find it is the greedy bitches that start this habit, then find it hard to stop.

Vitamin E is very useful for muscle tone and, with selenium and zinc, it enhances the reproductive system.

Vitamin K is needed for correct blood clotting and can be used when a dog has taken rat poison (such as Warfarin) which causes internal bleeding. Massive doses of K are injected in an attempt to save the dog's life. I mention this because Weimaraners have excellent scenting ability and forage out the most disgusting 'game' and poisoned rats can be amongst this 'game'.

Most dogs will receive the necessary vitamins and minerals in adequate proportions from their diet. As in humans, iron is needed to stop the dog becoming anaemic. Calcium and phosphorus are needed for growth and in a lactating bitch, but over-dosing should not be encouraged as it will lead to problems. Ask your vet or breeder which supplements are needed for your new puppy. Most breeders will include on the diet sheet the supplements they have given the puppy so far.

Whichever preparation you choose, make sure it is made by a reputable pharmaceutical company and that you read and comply with the instructions regarding dosages. I envisage no problems with rearing a sound, healthy puppy if his diet is supplemented sensibly. Indeed the only time you need be at all concerned about added vitamins or minerals is when your Weimaraner is very young or old, during the breeding programme, or sometimes if he appears to need a boost.

Fresh Meat

Feeding your dog fresh meat, as opposed to tinned, is very successful for many people but can be time-consuming and smelly. Beware of what is termed 'pet mince', because meat that is going off can cause all sorts of problems. Condemned meat should not be fed either – it may well be full of disease or antibiotics which make it unfit for human consumption. Pet mince may contain a lot of fat which is good for no one, man or beast.

Cooking meat is advisable, but make sure it reaches the correct temperature to kill any undesirable additives unless you know the exact source.

Tripe and paunch are good sources of protein. This is not the white gristly-looking product displayed in the butcher's window, but an untreated, grey, ugly-looking substance with the most appalling odour. I find feeding tripe to a house pet totally unacceptable. Not only does the home have the lingering aroma but the dog has foul breath and awful wind. However, it may work well for big kennels of working gundogs or the like.

Chicken is preferred by some but obviously this will be an expensive way to feed a big hungry breed like the Weimaraner. Minced chicken is literally minced whole chicken and contains crushed bones. It worries me because of the potential viruses it can also contain. Make sure you thaw frozen chicken properly. Lamb is good for dogs, either the tripe or breast, but it is fiddly and fatty, as is the head.

Fish and chicken are useful when a dog has been unwell. They are light and easily digested and are good for an old dog who needs a little spoiling when his digestive system is no longer what it was.

Whatever fresh meat you decide upon, always make sure you balance it with a good quality biscuit. More and more people are becoming health conscious today and are thinking in the same terms when feeding their dog. Manufacturers are now making high quality wholemeal biscuits, providing a greater choice of mixer.

Mixer is important because if the dog eats only meat he will not digest his food properly and this will give him diarrhoea. It will also increase his intake of protein to high above his needs, thus enhancing the possibility of making him hyperactive. A Weimaraner needs no encouragement in this.

Complete Foods

If you use a complete food, think before adding that bit of chicken, mince or tinned food to give it flavour. Complete means just that. It seems silly to me that a firm has spent thousands of pounds to achieve the correct balance of nutrients, just to have the balance ruined by some 'well-meaning' dog owner, who then worries that the food doesn't seem to be doing his dog any good.

The range of complete food on the market is vast. It may be helpful to ask the breeder's advice. See what he recommends and why, or ask friends who have healthy, fit, well-mannered dogs of a similar size. A Yorkshire Terrier should not have the same diet as a Weimaraner, for instance.

If you decide on a complete food, work out what suits you, taking into consideration practical feeding, cost, palatability and what you feel at ease with. Go to your retailer and discuss feeding with him. He will know better than anyone what each food contains and what it will do for your dog.

Clockwise from the top: wholemeal mixer biscuit; crunchy cob biscuit mixer; small mixer biscuit; Chubb, moist meat and cereal in a plastic sausage; complete expanded; complete flake type food; good quality tinned meat to use with mixer.

Complete foods come in various forms. Some are in the form of mixed flakes of cereal and chunks of dried meat, and end up looking like a museli breakfast cereal. These can be fed dry or soaked, or just mixed with water to retain the crunch but make the powder content more palatable. Most Weimaraners take to this way of feeding, but of course it can be messy mixing it in water.

Other complete foods are 'expanded' and come in a dry, crisp, nut pellet, or whatever shape the manufacturers come up with. These can be fed soaked or wet but are best if fed dry – there is no mixing and no smell. If it suits you and your dog, it is a very easy way to feed as long as you make sure that there is always clean water available.

Whatever way you decide to feed your Weimaraner, stick to it. We love variety in our diet: dogs are better with stability. Our dogs have the same diet every day of their lives and this enables them to maintain peak condition.

Milk

Cow's milk is the obvious choice for your dog but is very different from the bitch's milk, being lower in the protein and fat that the puppy needs. The nearest thing to the bitch's milk, other than a powdered bitch milk substitute, is ewe's milk, and agricultural stockists will have a powdered substitute designed for lambs. The one problem is that it usually comes in a big sack and therefore is impractical for one puppy. A powdered bitch's milk substitute is available from pet retailers or vets and this is far better than using cow's milk. Another alternative is goat's milk, which is not as good as bitch's or ewe substitute milk, but is useful because it is allergy free. If you use a powdered milk make sure you are accurate in measuring the dilution rate and read all instructions carefully.

Teaching Your Dog Proper Eating Habits

Always feed your puppy in the same place with his own dish and on his own, without distractions. Puppies are inquisitive, none more so than Weimaraners and if you put their food down and stand to watch them eat, they will get into the very bad habit of eating a little, then coming to see what you are doing, then having a little more and then coming back for a cuddle.

You might worry about him not eating and give him more at his next meal time to compensate. You might add something tasty, which he will eat excitedly. Consequently you are beginning to form a vicious circle. If you worry and tempt him, he, being very bright, will play up at feeding time, knowing it will affect you and ultimately lead to treats.

So don't overfeed him, put his dish down, then leave the room and shut the door, taking away his prime distraction. After ten minutes go in, take what he has left and dispose of the remains. If he hasn't cleaned his dish and the food is not left he will be more ready for his next meal. If you leave the food there it is essentially giving him for lunch what he left at breakfast, which isn't very appetising.

In the wild his natural instinct is to eat or die, because he doesn't know where or when he will get his next meal. By domesticating the dog, we have taken that instinct away to a certain extent, which is why, if we allow it, the dog will become fussy and dictate what he wants to eat.

Weimaraners are notorious thieves when it comes to food and are often very greedy. I have heard extraordinary tales of Weimaraners opening the fridge or getting into the sack of dog food and gorging themselves with, remarkably, no ill effects. How to cure a greedy Weimaraner is one of the great unanswered questions. You must get into the habit of not leaving food about and locking fridge doors. A locking catch can be purchased specifically for this purpose. You must also anticipate his actions.

Many reasons are given for why dogs are overweight, such as spaying or some obscure medical complaint. However, the real reason, in the majority of cases, is overfeeding.

If you have a dog who appears hungry and you hate to see him always asking for food, try substituting carrot or cabbage for more fattening biscuits. Carrots give the dog something to chew on and fill him up with nothing else, so he won't put on weight nor will he always feel ravenous.

We always feed adult Weimaraners two meals a day rather than one. One reason for this is that it is not unheard of for Weimaraners to suffer from Gastric Torsion or bloat, which invariably kills. It is not known why a dog suddenly suffers from this terrible condition (described in Chapter 10) but gorging on one meal, in my opinion, may be a contributory factor. Another reason is that a full twenty-four hours between meals seems a little unkind. Even with a greedy dog who puts weight on easily, I would rather feed two small meals than one bigger one.

Always feed at about the same time each day. Dogs are creatures of habit and they are much happier and settled in their eating if the same pattern is maintained. Fresh clean water should be available at all times for your dog.

The one exception to allowing free access to water is as an aid to housetraining. If a puppy finds it difficult to go all night without wetting the floor, one remedy is to restrict water after tea. He relieves himself last thing and having had no water to drink since early evening, is able to go through the night more easily. As he grows up he will gain greater bladder control and later water may be left down at all times.

Bowls

Obviously whatever you decide to feed your dog, you must consider his food and water dish. Weimaraners are strong, greedy characters so I would recommend investing in stainless steel bowls. Ceramic and enamel will probably be picked up in the dog's teeth and thrown around when he has finished eating with disastrous results not only to the bowl but also to the dog if sharp fragments of the broken bowl cut and damage him.

Plastic bowls can be chewed by determined Weimaraners and pieces of bowl, if swallowed, can cause problems and large vet fees. Aluminium bowls look harmless enough but this metal is soft and I have heard of a dog who ate his aluminium bowl.

Never feed a dog from a human utensil, be it the baked-on stew pan or your own dinner plate. Although this is a matter of choice, remember that the cute, clean, appealing-looking puppy who starts this habit will grow into a dog who will sit expectantly, drooling around the dinner table, even if guests are present, and will complain loudly if he is locked away.

For hygienic reasons feed him from his own bowls and put all leftovers in a dish to be added to his meal later, so he doesn't start begging. Also invest in utensils for him alone, especially a tin opener.

The Feeding Regime

After a week or two of following the breeder's guidelines you can slowly introduce your own feeding regime. Your puppy will probably need to be fed four meals a day when you first take him home. These will consist of two milky feeds and two meat feeds.

Breakfast will usually consist of a breakfast cereal designed for humans soaked with milk. Any calcium or mineral supplement can be given at this time. He is hungry at this meal and if the supplement is a powder and can be added to the food he will usually clean his dish rapidly and get all the additives he needs. If the supplement is in tablet form, it should be given at the same time every day, to reduce the chance of you forgetting.

Lunch should be one of the meat-orientated feeds. We advise a tinned feed and mixer especially designed for puppies. Some breeders swear by pitchard and/or fresh minced meat. However, if the diet is too rich, the puppy will develop loose motions to excrete the imbalance, which will put excessive wear on his intestines. For tea give him a meat-type feed again.

At about four months of age, depending on the puppy, lunch and tea can be merged to reduce the number of meals to three daily. When this occurs, change breakfast from the milky feed to a meat-type feed, so that the puppy has two meat meals, one at each end of the day.

Supper is usually in the form of rice pudding or semolina; continue this feed using your judgement. If the puppy is hungry and needs this feed, continue it for a number of months. If he is consistently fouling his sleeping area, consider reducing it or feeding it earlier to combat this problem.

Remember a Weimaraner is a fast-growing, athletic breed. He is not prone to putting on weight excessively as some breeds are, so you can afford to have your puppy become chunky rather than lean. If by chance he then catches a bug or goes off his food for some reason, he will not suffer too badly. A Weimaraner will naturally fine down when he reaches eight months or so. He might go through a stage where he looks rather like a Whippet, but this is a stage which he will grow out of. If you have kept him rather on the lean side he will not have the reserves to call on when he suddenly puts on a spurt of growth.

Different breeds have different requirements. For instance, a Labrador or Golden Retriever is prone to put on weight easily and must be watched as this weight can be hard to shift and can lead to health problems. If the vet tells you not to let your Weimaraner get too fat, he may be working on the assumption that all large gundogs are made the same and have the same requirements. This is most definitely not the case.

When you have decided which diet suits your dog and lifestyle, stick to it. If for some reason you feel the need to change the food, introduce the new method of feeding gradually to avoid upset digestion. His body needs time to adjust, so give the new food a chance by sticking to it for at least a couple of weeks.

Often Weimaraners go through a stage, usually in adolescence, when, despite your initial training, they become picky eaters. This is a form of testing you. Don't pamper to your dog's whims; have the attitude that you really don't care if he eats or not and he will soon revert to his hearty eating regime.

Bones

One thing I haven't mentioned is bones – if in doubt, don't. Bones can be useful for keeping the teeth and jaws clean and marrow bones help stimulate the gastric juices, but the wrong bone can do more harm than good. Only give your dog the big knuckle bones or marrow bones and never sharp, splintering chop bones or cooked chicken and rabbit bones, which can be deadly.

Small bones that can be swallowed and cause blockages should be avoided at all costs. You can purchase at a good pet supplier's sterilised bones, which are natural white bones and when gnawed on crumble instead of splinter, making them ideal for dogs of all ages.

Storage

It is more economical to buy food for your Weimaraner in bulk. Make sure, if you do, that you have the correct facilities to store the food, otherwise you could be encouraging vermin or might end up throwing musty, damp food away. If feeding a flake, complete or expanding dry food, a plastic dustbin will probably solve storage problems. It will accommodate a normal twenty kilo sack of food and, with the lid on, will keep thieves out. Unless you have an epidemic of mice, they shouldn't come to bother the bin, but get a metal one if they do.

Tinned foods need dry conditions otherwise they will rust and burst, become inedible and making a mess of the whole area. Remember that tins of dog food have a shelf life just like tins for human consumption. Nutrients deteriorate in all feeds after the sell-by date.

I would never consider feeding fresh meat or tripe without a dog-meat-only freezer. If left out even for a short period the meat will become fly blown and inedible. You need to segregate dog food for health reasons and tripe could taint other foods. A secondhand freezer in the garage should suffice.

4 Training

A good old Yorkshire saying goes, 'You never get ought out if you don't put ought in', and this sums up the training of a Weimaraner. When you pick up your puppy, that is when training should begin. This is best done when the puppy is seven to eight weeks of age. If you leave getting your puppy too late, it will make your job of training all the harder.

The Weimaraner has a wonderful ability to learn, even at this early age, and often one of the most worrying aspects of early training, from the new owner's point of view, is the fact that you find yourself saying 'NO' and issuing a short, sharp smack all the time.

If the puppy needs reprimanding, that one firm 'NO' and very sharp smack must always be followed up by praise when he has stopped his misdemeanour. Be clear and concise and the response will be so quick and the lesson learned with such speed that you will marvel at your puppy's intelligence, and find that the 'NO' becomes less necessary and the praise more so.

Travelling

Some dogs get terribly travel sick, while others don't – the breed does not seem to make a difference. The one thing about Weimaraners is that they love to be with you, so they like being in the car when you are there.

If your puppy is travel sick, don't feed him when you get home. Leave him a few hours for his tummy to settle. If he has been really poorly just give him a very small drink of water perhaps every hour to start with, otherwise he can have water freely.

Take the puppy with you on short nice journeys to start with. If your dog gets travel sick, the best thing you can give him is Sea Legs, the travel sickness tablets for humans. Your vet cannot prescribe anything better. All he can give you is a sedative, which is not much use if you are taking your dog for a long walk or to a show.

Travel sickness is often the puppy's first experience of being sick, so when he sees a car he immediately thinks 'I'm going to be sick again', and he is. If you can break this chain he will grow out of being sick very quickly. If you have a poor traveller, give him a Sea Legs tablet an hour or so before the journey. Continue to give him a tablet for a few journeys after he is happy in the car, just to be on the safe side.

When you first get a puppy and he hasn't had his inoculations, the breeder and vet will advise you not to take him out to a public place, like a park or the street, where dogs carrying disease are roaming free or where unvaccinated dogs are prevalent. Your puppy should be socialised though. If you are going to visit your mother or a friend who either doesn't have a dog or has a dog which is fully vaccinated, then take your puppy with you. By doing this he will realise that not all car journeys are traumatic. If he is going to see someone nice who spoils him a little and gives him treats he will soon look forward to the journey.

If you have a hatchback car or an estate, after the initial journey home, when you go out with the puppy in the car, always take someone with you, if possible. The person can talk to him and reassure him and if he is popped in the hatch or estate part, the other person can act as dog guard and stop him climbing over the seat. This is safer for him, he won't be thrown about the car and it will help him to learn that he is allowed only in the rear of the car. If you are persistent with this from the beginning there is every possibility that he may never need a dog guard and will stay happily in the rear on his own.

It can be a good idea if you are out in the car for an hour or so to take your Weimaraner with you. Remember to exercise the dog before leaving him for any length of time or you will be asking for trouble. If he is well exercised and tired he will curl up in the car and rest contentedly until you return.

In summer or cold weather leave your dog at home and don't take any chances. Very cold weather can be harmful to a dog as car insulation is not good; a car in hot weather turns into an oven very quickly and a dog can die from the heat and dehydration.

Sleeping Arrangements

If the new puppy is to live in the house and he is the only dog in the family, an indoor kennel is particularly useful. This is a large wire cage which is collapsible and can be stored out of the way when not in use. It has a plastic tray in the base and a front-opening door which can be fastened shut or left open at your discretion.

The indoor kennel should be erected in a quiet, draught-proof place. Ideally it should have a piece of Vetbed or similar warm puppy-proof bedding inside, so that the puppy is warm, comfortable and safe, and not able to foul the kitchen or lounge carpet or to chew or destroy anything. Vetbed is a type of synthetic sheepskin which reflects the body heat and therefore will keep the puppy warm. It is virtually indestructible and also

The indoor kennel. Purchase one large enough for the adult Weimaraner to grow into.

non-toxic, so that if a persistent puppy does manage to chew a corner and eat it he will come to no harm. Another plus to Vetbed is that if a puppy fouls or wets his bed, it can be clean and dry in no time as it is easily washed.

A puppy needs a sense of security and if he has a place of his own where he can go when he wants to rest or when he needs to escape he will be very happy in a short length of time. However, persistence is needed to convince him that by putting him in a kennel and shutting the door, you are not being cruel but are doing it for him. When you have settled him down for the night and made sure all his needs are accounted for, turn the light out, shut the door, and put cotton wool in your ears!

Virtually all puppies will cry to some extent. My advice is to let them. Your puppy will eventually stop and settle down if left alone and it is the best way if you, and the neighbours, can stand it. He will tire and drop off, although when he wakes he will probably pipe up again, but stick with it. In two or three days, possibly less, he will realise that at night we sleep or rest quietly, and he can have attention only when you say, not when he demands it.

Some people are quite happy for the new puppy to sleep in their bedroom, and if this is what you want, fine. He may, of course, decide to get on or even in the bed in the middle of the night and no one will ever sleep normally again.

Everyone must decide what is best for them, but remember, if you give in that first night, with the intention of not letting it become a habit, you have

Clockwise from left front: washable fabric bed with detachable cushion; quilted bed with washable cover; waterproof beanbag with detachable washable cover; moulded solid plastic bed; Vetbed, fluffy on outside; non-chewable backing which allows water to pass through.

lost the battle. He will not easily go down into the kitchen, the howling and barking will be far louder and will persist far longer than if you start as you mean to go on.

An outside kennel with a run is another alternative. The expense can be great, but it can be reduced considerably if you are at all handy at DIY.

The cost of a 4 ft x 6 ft garden shed is not too astronomical and it can be easily adapted. The shed needs lining, with cavity-filled polystyrene or other insulation. Either an insulated raised bed with Vetbed or a boarded back half, which can be filled with deloused straw or shredded paper, should be made so that the dog has a place to snuggle down.

A side door is advisable, preferably with a stable door, so the top may be left open for ventilation in hot weather. Be sure to put an internal wire door in if you intend to leave the top door open, otherwise it won't be long before he can and will jump out. Also make sure you have secure fastenings, not only for when the door is shut but also for when you plan to leave it open. A window is not advisable unless weld mesh is put over the inside, otherwise when the puppy grows, being a curious animal, he will jump at the window to see what is going on and will smash it. Weimaraners can be clumsy.

A bob hole inserted into the front of the shed allows the dog out into a very secure run. It need not be elaborate as it is not meant to be used for exercise, but to allow the dog out into the fresh air and to potter about.

Make sure, if you have a run, that you either flag or pave the run area. This is a good idea for two reasons: first, if your Weimaraner gets bored he will try to dig his way out and flagging will stop this. Secondly, the area can be cleaned easily, therefore preventing the build-up of faeces and smell, which attracts flies.

The run itself needs to be of strong gauge weld mesh. The interlocking plastic-covered wire is no good: a Weimaraner will soon pull or chew a hole in it and escape. Leave him a bowl of water, some biscuits and a marrow or sterilised bone and he will be content when left.

If you do decide on an indoor kennel or an outside kennel and run, make sure that the puppy gets used to that environment from an early age, preferably as soon as you take him home.

Your Role as Pack Leader

A dog is a pack animal, so if you want to live successfully with a Weimaraner don't ever forget this. I am amazed that 'kind' people think that humanising a dog is a good thing.

A dog feels most secure in a pack situation with a leader to look up to. Sometimes he may wish to challenge the pack leader, but that is a different story. Treating a dog as you would a child reduces his pack instincts and leaves him vulnerable and on the defensive.

We always introduce a puppy we intend to keep into the pack as soon as the other pups go. The older dogs always seem to know how far to go with a baby so as not to hurt him. If the pack leader is chewing a bone, the other dogs don't interfere. It is an unwritten rule, but a puppy has to learn for himself. He will invariably trot up to inspect what is going on and may decide that the bone looks tasty. The older dog will growl to warn him off but will not hurt him. He may, if the puppy takes it too far, snap at him, sometimes making him scream in shock, but to this day I have never found a mark on the puppy.

When your puppy is eating a chew, for instance, make a point of going up and taking it away; you might pretend to eat it, or simply hold it and talk to the puppy. After a while give it back to him and praise him for being good. If he growls he must be punished. Smack him and say 'NO' very firmly.

Some people say that it is only natural for a puppy to growl in protest at having his own chew taken from him. If his litter mate was doing the taking, he would be standing up for his rights. However, it is most certainly not his right when someone higher in the pecking order is involved. You take on the role of pack leader in this type of situation. Don't make the mistake of letting a puppy have superiority over you as it could cause trouble later on, especially with children.

Some people think it is amusing to see a small puppy guarding his chew or dish of food – they won't when he grows to 70 lb or 80 lb and guards his favourite chair. A puppy thinks of you as his parent initially and must learn

to respect you as such; he must not treat you as his equal or inferior. If he starts to be aggressive and gets away with it he will get worse as he grows older.

It is not cruel to lay out a set of rules which must be obeyed. The rules are there for everyone's well being, not only yours but the dog's. It is inconsistency which ultimately causes pain and distress. From the start make sure your dog knows what he can and cannot do. Weimaraners are very bright and learn things very quickly if they are taught in a way they can understand clearly.

Housetraining

Once you have your Weimaraner puppy home, one of the first things to do is to housetrain him. A puppy is a bit like a baby in that he gains more control over his bodily functions as time goes on. He gains this control much sooner than a baby and at eight weeks begins to know or learn where he is allowed to go to the toilet and where he is not. Instinctively he will not want to defecate where he lives or sleeps. He might, not by choice but because he could not get where he wanted. Right from the beginning, think for him: learn to read the signs. When he wakes up, a puppy usually wants to relieve himself, so pick him up immediately, take him outside and encourage him to go, using the same words every time. If, for instance, you say 'Be good', he will go when he hears the words 'Be good' if you are persistent with the command every time you take him out. When he has relieved himself, praise him and pet him to show how pleased you are with him. Another time he may want to relieve himself is after he has eaten. Again, take him straight out and encourage him to go.

When he is playing a game with the children and he stops and starts to potter about, sniffing as he goes, often in decreasing circles, get him out quickly as it is a sure sign. Stay with him while he is outside. This can get very boring if he forgets why he has been taken out. Be patient because he will remember eventually and get on with it.

If he has an accident, pick him up and say a disapproving 'NO'. Take him straight outside and encourage him to go; even if it is too late he will get the general idea. Don't rub his nose in it and get excited, because that will worry him and he won't perform for you at all in case you repeat your show of disapproval. He will be more hurt if you quietly and quickly show your disapproval, because he does not like to be ignored.

When he makes a mistake, clean it up with disinfectant as quickly as possible to remove the scent and stain, as well as for hygienic reasons. If the spot is clean, he will not be able to remember where he went before and will not consider going there again. A good way to remove toilet stains and smells is to squirt the stain with soda water as soon as possible after mopping up.

One method of training a puppy is to put newspaper on the floor near the outside door, gradually moving it outside as he gets accustomed to using it. However, I find this can confuse him. One minute he is allowed to perform in the house, the next he is not. He cannot be expected to differentiate between paper in the house and paper outside. It is far better to make the rules clear, right from the start. Inside no, outside yes. Otherwise you might end up with more than you bargained for when you are reading the Sunday paper on the floor!

If at all possible it is best to use one door to take him outside. As he becomes familiar with the procedure, he will go to the door himself to ask to be let out. When he does, drop everything and take him out; there is no room for manoeuvre on this point, it is the sign that you are winning.

Obviously night training is another problem. Restricting his intake of fluid later in the day can help. Confining him to a small place, such as an indoor kennel, to sleep will also help. It will encourage him to wait or to bark for you, as no dog willingly fouls his bed.

People in desperation have resorted to taking the puppy upstairs to resolve the problem – a drastic measure and one that is not easily reversed as he will not take kindly to being left downstairs again when clean.

After a few months, he will be in complete control of his bodily functions. Weimaraners are usually clean by nature. Our males would never dream of cocking their leg in the house. It is interesting to note that a puppy that has been kennelled outside, and therefore not housetrained, at seven or eight months can come inside the house and automatically expect to go out to the toilet. Kennel bitches that are brought in to be whelped will instinctively want to be clean and will never do anything in the house.

Jumping Up

A dog that jumps up all the time is not being wilfully naughty, he is just pleased to see you. He wants attention, and the bit of you that tends to give him that attention with kind reassuring words and gestures, is the head and face. His only way to get to that part is by jumping up. He must be taught that this is wrong. You may not mind when he is a clean puppy, but when he is a dirty grown dog stopping him from jumping up is considerably harder, as well as being confusing to him because you are changing the rules.

The best way to teach him not to jump up is to get hold of him firmly and make a definite action that puts him on the floor. For instance, firmly take hold of the skin on each side of his neck and physically put him down or lift your knee into his chest. As you are performing this action, say very firmly in a stern voice, 'NO, DOWN'. While you are holding him down, tell him what a clever puppy he is, pet and praise him. It won't take long for him to realise that you are pleased when he stays down but not when he climbs up. If he jumps up and you wave him to one side, flapping your arms about, he will not understand the command and will react accordingly.

Friends and neighbours can be a problem in training the puppy not to jump up. They must respect your wishes in training the pup or all your efforts will be in vain. Your dog should be able to meet strangers without becoming over-excited. If you have to put the dog in another room, it will only make the problem worse. Therefore, ask nicely but firmly that people do not encourage him to jump up. This can be achieved by visitors ignoring the dog until they are settled in the house, with you restraining him. Position yourself between him and the visitor, and give the pup a short, sharp smack and firm 'NO' if he misbehaves.

When the excitement of the arrival has subsided, let the puppy go and say hello sensibly to the visitor. This procedure becomes very time-consuming, but if done properly and consistently you will reap the benefits.

When he has said hello and the visitors have petted him for a while, ask the puppy to come away and settle down. Perhaps a good way to do this is for you to sit calmly on the floor with him and stroke him gently; carry on the conversation with the visitors, ignoring the puppy, and let him settle off to sleep. If you can persevere with this calming approach when people come around, you will encourage puppy not to become too excited.

Toys

After establishing your puppy in his new home and into a sleeping routine, the next step is for him to learn what is his to play with or chew. It is best to purchase some toys especially for him. Your local pet shop will have a good selection, although be wary of some. Weimaraners think squeaky toys are fun, but you will reach screaming point with the incessant noise. Weimaraners are notorious for their determination and can squeak for hours on end. It is wise to buy more than one toy but only one with a squeak, for the sake of your family's sanity.

Make sure that all toys and chews are non-toxic and are not easily chewed into bits, because if they are eaten they can cause health problems. Hide chews are a good choice for Weimaraners, as are the compressed minced hide chews, all of which come in various shapes and sizes. Such chews, if swallowed whole, represent no hazard to the dog, as they should dissolve in his digestive system without causing any blockages.

Dogs, in general, love the shavings that the farrier leaves behind after shoeing the horse. These are in small pieces and create no problems.

Whole, cleaned cow hooves can be bought from the pet shop; however, I would not recommend them for Weimaraners. One of the best bones on the market is the sterilised knuckle bone described in Chapter 3. It helps promote healthy teeth and gums and although it can be quite large, it is useful for puppies to chew when teething.

A toy that is inexpensive and gives hours of fun is an old sock stuffed full of other old socks and knotted securely. It is safe to throw and can be played with safely. It is often remarked that it can be the cheapest and easiest toys that give the most pleasure, and the sock is no exception.

Playing with Your Puppy

One of the greatest pleasures in life for a puppy is for you to play with him. We teach our youngsters that this should be done outside, never in the house. As with children, the adrenalin begins to flow, they get excited and things get knocked over and broken. If your puppy thinks that this sort of behaviour is permitted in the house, then it can lead to other problems. He will generally become unruly, disobedient and wilful, thinking that if he can behave badly with you then he can do the same when you are not there. All of which leads to a destructive, out-of-control dog, which you will wish you had never bought.

While enjoying playing with your Weimaraner remember always to keep him under control. Don't ever allow him to bite at you, even in fun. If he wants to bite, as puppies naturally do, pick up a stick and let him bite that or take the old stuffed sock and throw it, drawing his attention away from chewing on anything. If you allow him to bite in play as a baby, when he grows he will automatically snap or bite if reprimanded. As an adult he will have a jaw like a vice and teeth like 'Jaws'; this could lead to you being shocked or injured. He will be able to sense your apprehension when he grabs your arm and that will give him mental superiority. If you discipline him again in the future, he will remember your previous apprehension when he grabbed you and do it again, though this time it will be a bit harder, and before you know it, you will have a dog that bites. He must be taught right from the start that such behaviour is not permitted in any form.

When playing rough games with your dog, don't allow him to climb on your back or jump about wrapping his legs around you. You will end up with the dog becoming sexually excited and demonstrative. If you think the game is getting out of hand, stop it and draw the dog's attention to something else he will find interesting. Such behaviour is practically impossible to rectify in an adult, so stop it when he is a puppy.

Over-excitement is usually the cause of such displays, so avoid it. Becoming upset yourself and punishing the dog will only serve to confuse him and could make him worse. Divert his attention by giving him something else to do that will quieten him down, therefore removing the problem. By hitting him and going into a hysterical frenzy, you will only upset him and may find that this sort of behaviour will lead to him being unwilling to serve a bitch in the future, if required.

Children and Dogs

You must always teach dogs to behave properly with children, without exception. Likewise, children should be taught to respect dogs and not to abuse them.

A family with a new baby should not have to contemplate parting with their dog simply because of the new arrival. However, you should be aware that Weimaraners are devoted and possessive dogs and will feel jealous of the love and attention the newcomer receives. Make sure that your dog is not ignored completely.

Try to have a break from the dog occasionally, otherwise you might have trouble when you do have to leave him in kennels or for the day, if you get a job or go on holiday. Short, regular use of the indoor kennel prevents such a problem before it arises.

If a new baby arrives, give the dog your attention when the baby is sleeping and pop him in his kennel when you are busy with the baby. The break will do you both good.

As the child grows it might be easier to put the dog in his kennel while the child runs around – at least until she has learned that dogs' eyes are not for poking and their tails and ears are not to be pulled. Even constant hugging by a child can distress a Weimaraner and not knowing how else to deal with such a situation, he could resort to growling at the child. Remember that the dog needs to be considered too.

Don't leave the dog and child together unattended. If you have a free minute, sit down with them and let the child stroke the dog properly. This way no resentment will build up between the two and the dog will learn that the child is to be loved.

Lead Training

Before you take your puppy to the park he has to be lead trained. There are a variety of leads available and everybody has their personal favourite.

I always walk train a Weimaraner on a choke chain. The small chain choker with a handle is ideal. This is very easy to handle when on the dog, as the small links slip easily. They are too small to snatch at the hair on the dog's neck, and neither cause discomfort nor mark the coat. The short handle means the dog can't pull, but is forced to heel.

If you use a long lead, the dog might pull as he wanders away. If you need to check him you have yards of lead to gather up before you produce any effect at all. The long lead gives you less leverage and therefore your arm will ache.

The large link, curb chain chokers are not suitable for two reasons: first, the large link chain doesn't slip back through the ring (round) link easily and can stick, so that instead of slipping back to tighten around the dog's neck it can wedge on the ring link and will remain loose on his neck. If he pulls back sharply in this situation, the choker will come off his head. Secondly, it is far more likely to cut and pull the hair round his neck, causing discomfort and a dark line on his coat. This will be detrimental if you wish to show him.

Rope or nylon chokers are also available. These are fine if the dog is trained properly. Rope chokers are useful if you are field trialing. Because they are soft they won't hurt your hand when wet, and they are quiet and lightweight, so they can be carried by you easily when the dog is loose and hunting. Nylon chokers are good to use when showing. Because they are flat they don't interrupt the line of the dog when he is placed in the show position. They are quickly pulled up round his neck and you waste little time when asked to move him up in front of the judge. Both are easily slipped off and put in your pocket when not required. A nylon lead is available with a push-down clip, but I find that it can slip back if the dog resists and come over the dog's head, in a similar way to the big link choker.

Many people simply use a leather collar and lead. As dogs are required by law to wear a collar and name tag, this is practical. The initial training should still be done with a choke chain though, for ease of checking.

The best collar for a puppy to wear continuously is the cheapest, as they have to be replaced regularly until the puppy is fully grown. When he is an adult, a rolled leather or soft cotton web collar is ideal. They won't damage the coat the way a cheap hard leather collar will.

If you put the puppy on a lead in the garden and coax him to move before he is old enough to go out on the road, you will have excellent results. It is a kind and gentle way of achieving the result you want without causing stress. Once the puppy has had his inoculations, he can be walked on the pavement. Try and take him out when there is little traffic about; he will then be able to accustom himself to traffic gradually and will not be frightened by it.

Remember for his first few walks to choose somewhere near that he will find interesting so that he will be eager to return, even if he has to suffer the lead to get there.

Teaching Your Puppy His Name

A puppy should answer to his name quickly. The easiest way to teach him is if you have a one-to-one relationship with him. The greatest stumbling block is a lot of children, all shouting at him. His name becomes a noise amongst noises and means nothing to him, and therefore he won't respond to it.

Initially only call his name when you are sure he will come to you. For example, if he is bored with the game he is playing and looking for something exciting to do, crouch down to his level and call his name, encouraging him to come to you. You will find he romps towards you. When you give him his food dish, call his name and he will respond to the message of the food. If you see him setting off in your direction, call him by name and he will come to you. He will very quickly realise that if he hears his name he is to go to you. He will not respond as quickly if he is doing something exciting when you call him. At first, only use his name when you are sure you have his attention and he will respond positively. If he is in the garden and trotting after something in the opposite direction, don't call him if you want him; run after him and only say his name as you pick him up. You will reap the benefit of this name training after he has had his inoculations and you take him to the park.

Walking Your Dog

On the first few visits to the outside world he will stick to you for protection and support. When he goes off exploring and you call him back, he will return rapidly. He needs you and won't risk your disapproval when he is unsure of his surroundings. When he gets used to them, however, you might not get such a quick response. You must learn to read the situation and pre-empt his reactions, avoiding trouble before it happens.

When he is five or six months old and you go to the park, you must be able to visualise what is going to happen next. If he sees a man and a dog coming over the hill in the distance, being bold and fun loving, he will want to rush over to play. You might call him back, but he doesn't want to come to you. He could be bitten by the other dog, even though his owner has him on a lead, and then run off frightened and in pain.

The next day you will be aware of the dog on the hill and will put your dog on his lead. As the other dog approaches, your Weimaraner might think, 'I was bitten yesterday, but I'll get in first today', so he growls. You then have the makings of a vicious Weimaraner.

Remember the Breed Standard reads, 'Friendly but fearless', so he could end up with a bad reputation through no fault of his own. He might even read your apprehension and growl at the other dog to protect you, because he thinks you are afraid of it, not the situation.

Avoid such a situation happening by putting your dog on his lead as soon as *you* see a man with a dog, then they can pass each other in a friendly, relaxed manner. If the dog turns out to be friendly, then you can decide if you want them to play, but remember that as pack leader it is your choice, not his.

Your dog should not be allowed to rush up to strange people when he is out. They might not like dogs or may even be frightened of them. They have the right to walk in the park unmolested, as have you. If they wish to make friends with him, they have the choice of coming up to you to ask if they may. You know he is friendly but they don't. It will be much better for the reputation of all dogs if yours is well mannered and controlled when he is outside his home.

Many owners of male dogs, especially Weimaraners, say their dog is fantastic with people and even bitches, but because he was bitten by a dog when young, he is now on his guard with male dogs and can be nasty. I once challenged one owner who said this; when he thought about it, he realised it was his own negligence that created the situation and his fault, therefore, that he had a wary adult dog. Ninety per cent of such cases are due to the owner's negligence.

As a responsible dog owner, you should always look to promoting your dog in a good light. A little thought goes a long way towards this. You should never allow your dog to foul in public. If an accident happens where people could be in contact with it, you must clean it up with a poop scoop or something similar. Many responsible dog owners carry a supply of small plastic bags in their coat pocket and put their hand in the bag to pick up the excrement. Turn the bag inside out and put it inside another bag to avoid leakage, then you can dispose of it efficiently and hygienically. It isn't a very pleasant job, nor is putting your foot in a pile of dog excrement.

If, when you are housetraining your puppy, every time he performs you say 'Be clean', or some such phrase, he will, after a while, perform on command, in the same way as he responds to his name. This is useful when you take him out for the day or for a walk, as you will be able to take him to an isolated spot, which people don't frequent, to perform on the utterance of the magic words. This will save you from embarrassment later.

When I walk my dogs, as well as generally surveying the area as I walk, I often call a dog back to me for no particular reason. This serves to remind the dog that if I call he must come. If I use his name I always make sure that he comes right up to me, not just in my general direction. After patting him I will then let him go off again, or I may give him a biscuit, or even put him on the lead for a minute or two. Although I do different things with him every time I call him, I make sure that I always touch him.

One habit best avoided is only putting his lead on at the end of a walk. The dog will soon begin to realise what is happening and when the lead comes out, will disappear if he feels like extending his walk.

If, after all the correct training, you find when he is about twelve months old that he won't come when called, it is his version of the juvenile delinquent stage, when he is disobeying to be defiant, as teenagers do. If you cannot retrieve your dog without much effort, when you finally succeed, put him on the lead and make him walk to heel, obeying your commands until he responds instantly as in the initial training. Find a quiet spot and let him off the lead, making him stay thoroughly obedient and increasing his freedom all the time. Call him back, make a great fuss of him and give him a reward. He then understands that you are not amused at his disobedience, but approve of him when he is good. Only do this for a short time; don't push your luck.

It is said you should not punish a dog for coming back. I believe that if you are fair and clear in your punishment when you finally have him back, you will teach him why he has to obey you instantly. Do not be too hard, which will frighten him, but show your disapproval quietly and determinedly.

You must *never* call him back sweetly, then punish him, as this is inconsistent and will confuse him. He will then not trust you at all. If the only way to get him back is to call him sweetly, put him on his lead with a quiet pat and then ignore him for a short while. That will be as good a punishment as any, as he hates being ignored. The next time you take him off the lead, make sure there are no distractions, call him back sooner, and give him a reward. You must be particularly vigilant at this stage of development in a junior Weimaraner.

Common sense tells you if your pup is overtiring himself. Letting your puppy play outside to amuse himself is one thing, taking him for an hour long walk is another. Do not expect too much too soon.

Sheep

Weimaraners should never be allowed to wander; make the boundaries secure from the start. Being hunting dogs and very athletic, if allowed to roam free they will get up to all sorts of mischief.

A lot of Weimaraners live in the country, so sheep worrying is always a possibility. Most breeds are capable of sheep worrying, given the right conditions. Weimaraners are inherently more prone to it than other breeds. Once started, it is virtually impossible to curb. It is your responsibility to stop it from happening to start with, so don't blame the farmer for shooting your dog to protect his sheep or the dog for behaving instinctively.

Problems with Males

The trouble with male dogs starts at adolescence. It usually erupts at about eight to twelve months and gets worse unless curbed. The initial training of a male puppy is therefore especially important.

I often suggest to somebody having problems gaining respect from his dog that he get a riding crop. I think it is cruel to hit a dog with your hand or flap about with paper; it is much better to administer a short sharp lesson with the crop. A crop is ideal because it is twangy and stings, but does not inflict damage, as a stick or foot would do, and the dog will be under no illusions as to what it is for.

The crop is the ultimate weapon; if you train him properly and with authority, you should rarely have to resort to it. It is amazing how much the dog's manners improve when he sees you pick it up.

Boarding Kennels

Weimaraners generally react dreadfully to being kennelled. They eat well, play well, enjoy their walks and generally lose weight to the point where you can study their skeletons without the benefit of X-rays. I believe this is one reason why the breed is nicknamed the Grey Ghost, not just because of their ethereal colour.

The Weimaraner needs to be with you. He attaches himself to one person, although he will be friendly with all the family. One person will be the recipient of his undivided love and devotion and he misses her when left in kennels, which is why he loses weight. Although he will eat well, it is stress and worry that burn off the calories.

I find that feeding the dogs in kennels three times a day, walking with them and talking to them helps them settle and hold their weight much better. I can keep their weight on them for two weeks and suddenly they decide they can't stand the separation any longer and lose weight dramatically in a couple of days.

It is therefore a good idea to board your Weimaraner when he is young. He will adapt to it far more easily than when older. When he is boarded later on as an adult he will remember and accept the situation more readily, because he knows you will be returning for him.

You might find it easier to send him to relatives or friends, or even to have someone staying in your house to dog-sit him. Just remember that the time may come when you have no choice but to board him.

Weimaraners are very sensitive and mentally aware. I often think that although not ideal, a Weimaraner can cope well with less exercise than he really needs. He will not cope so well without the mental stimulation.

If you own a Weimaraner, you have a beautiful, intelligent, loyal friend who doesn't suffer fools gladly, so treat him as such. Give your dog the respect he deserves and it will be reciprocated.

Physical force should be a last resort when training Weimaraners. Don't start a training session if you are short of time as Weimaraners are notoriously stubborn. If you find tension and tempers rising when training your pup, stop. When you reach such a stage all your frustration and emotion will be passed on to the dog and he will become distressed. Nothing will be achieved at such a time, so forget the training and do something else while you let everything calm down.

5 Breeding

People tend to have an idealised view of being able to breed from their bitch. I am amazed by the number of enquiries I have for stud dogs. When asked why they want to breed from their bitch, the owners' inevitable reply is that they want to have the bitch spayed and feel she will be better for having had a litter of puppies first, or that she will be better for having a litter of puppies in general. However, they are not really doing it for the bitch, because what she has never had she will not miss.

Many people think it is the miracle cure for bitches who suffer regularly from false pregnancies, but in my experience this is not the case. A false pregnancy is indicated when the bitch becomes puffy, filling with fluid after her season. Her udder swells and she becomes lethargic and uninterested in playing with the other dogs. Showing her can be difficult at such times, because she appears unfit.

Many people want to have a litter of puppies because they think it will be hugely profitable. Money can be and is made out of breeding pedigree dogs including Weimaraners, but this is usually at great cost to the breed. Indiscriminate breeding is frowned upon and actively discouraged by people who have the best interest of the breed at heart, be they professional or lay people. In fact, it is this indiscriminate breeding, not interbreeding, which causes severe problems when breeding animals. The Weimaraner Club of Great Britain has a code of conduct for all members and if they do not adhere to it strictly they are banned from further membership to the Club.

Many professional dog breeders and showers feel it is wrong for a pet bitch to have a litter, that it ought to be left to the experts. However, many of these people, although full of enthusiasm, may produce sub-standard puppies as easily as a layman. You have to take advice from your peers. It is difficult to produce a good litter from excellent stock and practically impossible to do it from inferior stock. Indiscriminate breeding of inferior stock may produce a 'one off' good puppy on occasion.

Weimaraners are a lovely breed in the right hands and if the correct guidance is given over a long period of time to help the new owner through the various stages of development, both physical and mental. Breeding puppies needs lots of time, patience and money. Think carefully before you plan your litter.

If, at the end of your deliberations, you would still like to rear a litter of puppies from your bitch, you could easily have a litter of eight or more puppies. Will you be able to find homes for them? Are you an experienced enough owner to be able to discuss with prospective owners the pitfalls as well as joys of owning such a dog? Will you be able to explain to them how to cope with a male Weimaraner? Are you sure that you will be able to carry out a thorough and correct vetting procedure? Will you be able to cope if you have several puppies unsold at twelve weeks, eating you out of house and home, dispelling obnoxious waste everywhere and generally creating havoc? Can you afford the vet's fees if anything goes wrong, because pregnancy and associated illnesses are not usually covered by insurance? Will you be able to advertise them properly, as this is very expensive? What will happen if someone returns to you in eighteen months with an uncontrollable dog that they can no longer cope with or keep? Will you be able to do the right thing and find it a good home? If you decide to breed your bitch, you must feel confident that you are doing the right thing for yourself, the bitch and the future puppies.

The Bitch's Season

Your bitch has her first oestrous cycle any time after six months. If she has shown no sign of coming into season by eighteen months, consult your vet. He may advise giving her a hormone injection to bring her into season. There may be the possibility that she has malformed ovaries or indeed no ovaries at all. If this is the case, she will be unable to produce eggs to fertilise and, therefore, will be barren. If she is not barren, the hormone injection administered by your vet may well jolt your bitch into coming into season. You could mate her then, but I would leave it until she came into season naturally the next time.

Another method of bringing a bitch into season is to kennel her with bitches already in season. Breeders often find that their bitches tend to come into season at much the same time or follow each other into season.

You could in theory mate your bitch on her first season and every season thereafter, but this is not desirable. However, if she was not in good enough condition or would suffer from a pregnancy, she probably would not conceive. In reality, it is best to leave a maiden bitch until she is two years old before you mate her. By this time she will be physically strong and mature as well as mentally mature. This should enable her to be happy, healthy and contented, and therefore a good parent with a strong, healthy litter of youngsters.

If your bitch comes into season more often than every five months, or if there is an abnormal amount of blood, consult your vet. Bitches will continue to have seasons until they are very old. They can be fertilised as easily in old age as when they are young, and some even have been known to have their first litter at thirteen years of age, but this is not advisable.

A normal season starts with the swelling of the vulva, followed by a brownish-red discharge which quickly turns bright red. This is called day one of the season, although dogs start to take an interest in the bitch a week to ten days before this happens. Always watch your bitch carefully because she might act completely out of character and try to run off with any male she sees.

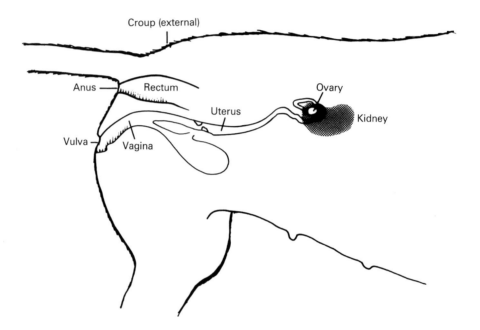

The heavy red discharge reduces to a light, clear discharge at about day eleven of the season and this is usually the time the bitch is ovulating and therefore considered to be ready for mating. After about fourteen days the discharge begins to dry up, but you must consider your bitch to be in season for the full twenty-one days or court disaster.

Weimaraner bitches can often show colour throughout the whole season. If you wish to have her mated you have to look for other signs of ovulation as well. When she is ready to be mated if you apply pressure to her croup she will swing her tail to one side and arch her back. She will also do this if you scratch the base of her tail. Her reaction is a good sign as to whether she is ready to mate or not.

A bitch usually looks in superb condition prior to coming into season. About three months after her season she will often lose her coat, it may look patchy and dull or she may lose condition and have a false, 'pseudo' or phantom pregnancy. The loss of coat is not as severe in the Weimaraner as it is in some other breeds.

It is not advisable to walk your dog when she is in season. You may end up fighting off rampant males and dragging your bitch home. Failing that, neighbourhood dogs may follow your scent home and queue up on your doorstep howling day and night. If you insist on exercising her, do it at an unsociable hour of the night and take her in the car so that she does not leave a trail right up to your door.

If you are a responsible owner you will not let your bitch escape during her season and get pregnant. Never let her out into the garden on her own, day or night. ALWAYS stay with her. It amazes me what dogs will do to get to bitches in heat, or vice versa.

Never assume that a dog is too large or too small to 'tie' with a bitch. When a bitch is ready to mate, she can be very accommodating. Likewise, never assume a male is too young. One six-month-old male mated his kennel mate and the result was ten puppies.

Various preparations are sold to disguise the odour of a bitch in season, which you should ask your vet about. However, many a wise old dog prick up their tails to those odours, knowing there must be a bitch in season somewhere.

It is much better to visit your vet and have him administer a hormonal treatment to stop the season happening altogether. This may take the form of tablets or injection. Accept your vet's advice, he knows best. Just be sure you take her quickly enough and keep her away from dogs until you are certain the hormones have worked. This course of action is time-consuming and expensive and has to be repeated at every season.

Spaying

If you don't want to breed your bitch, it is advisable to have her spayed. You must weigh up the pros and cons, but spaying can be a reasonable alternative. Some vets feel it is easier to spay a bitch while she is still immature, as her uterus will not be fully developed. I prefer to leave spaying until the bitch has had one full season; she may need her first season to mature her body fully. Early spaying might even hinder this process. If it is done after the first season the bitch will be young enough to cope with the stresses and strains involved with relative ease. It is far easier for a one year old to get over such an operation than a five year old, and it reduces the risk of any unwanted pregnancies.

Some people think bitches lose their personalities and vitality, becoming staid old ladies practically overnight. This is totally without foundation. Such a thing might happen as the bitch reaches maturity and settles down naturally, but it will be a coincidence and not connected to the operation itself. Often spayed bitches put on weight, but this is generally caused by overfeeding. Spaying is thought by some to lead to incontinence, although it has never been proved.

There is always an element of risk involved in any operation, although generally speaking the risk is slight with spaying. If you have no intention of breeding with your bitch, it is a wise solution to a life-long problem. If you show your bitch, Kennel Club regulations state that you may only spay her for medical reasons and The Kennel Club must be informed.

The First Litter

The best time for a bitch to have her first litter is between the ages of two and three: after two years, to allow your bitch time to mature physically and mentally, and before three years, so that she is young and fit, making whelping easier. A bitch should be bred from only when she is in superlative condition.

This is not to say that an older bitch will have any problems, but the risk is slightly greater, increasing as the bitch ages. It is not wise to mate a five-year-old maiden bitch. Likewise, I have seen a young bitch caught and mated at seven months on her first season. The litter was healthy enough, but it took a lot out of the bitch and she never grew on properly from there.

People often assume that by looking at a bitch they can tell if she will be a good brood. This is not necessarily the case. A good brood bitch in my interpretation is one that produces sound, healthy puppies and is a sensible mother who looks after her puppies well, both in milk production and caring. This good brood bitch must also be capable of passing on her good genetic qualities to her offspring.

When breeding, you should strive to improve; never go back to try to retrieve what you had in the past or stand still. You must be objective; do not blind yourself to the dog's faults. It often happens that an immensely successful dog or bitch will never produce good pups, either once or consistently, the reason being that they do not have good breeding behind them. Of course, there is an element of luck in breeding. You may produce a fine litter of pups by taking your bitch to a good champion dog, but this may not be the case every time.

On the other hand, you can mate a bitch with good breeding lines to a carefully chosen, well-bred dog, matching the pedigrees, cross-referencing good qualities with bad, making sure that what one is short of the other makes up for. You could have lovely pups but they might be untypical and therefore not suitable for showing. Find out how genes affect breeding – studying genetics helps the breeder to comprehend how and why traits are passed down to a puppy.

We were once told by a great dog man never to match up two extremes.

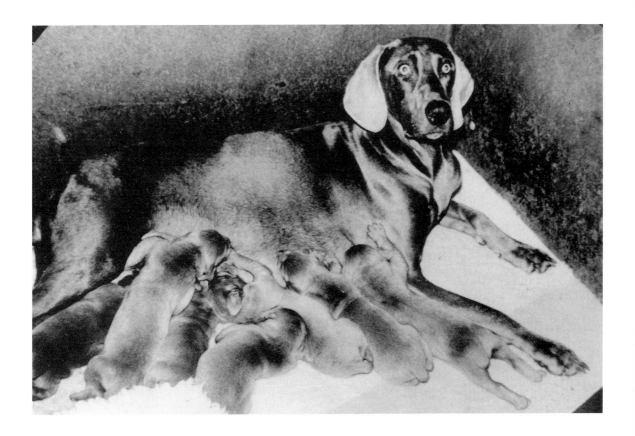

By this I mean a poor-headed bitch with a super-headed dog, or a big dog to a small bitch to increase the size of the pups. We were told that from such a mating we would have a mixture of pups, some with good heads, some with bad, some of good size and some too small. I have watched the results of such matings and invariably the great dog man is right. Opposites or extremes do not produce something in the middle. Remember compatibility is the key to success.

Sh. Ch. Hansom Hirondelle. 'Gemma' was bred by Dick Finch and owned by Denise Mosey. She is the record holder for the most Champion or Show Champion offspring – six. Many of these children have gone on to be the foundation behind winning lines today.

Choosing the Stud Dog

How do you choose the correct stud dog? The first steps are to listen to advice from people involved in the breed, especially at shows and field trials, study pedigrees with people knowledgeable about breeding Weimaraners and discuss what you want to achieve in the resulting puppies. Consequently, your advisers may suggest which dog's ancestors will enhance your bitch's ancestors.

As a novice it will be difficult for you to understand your bitch's pedigree and you will probably not know her ancestors personally. Look at a kennel that conforms to the Breed Standard as you interpret it. Go and talk to the owners of the strain that you admire. Make sure it is a kennel that has a good long strain that is consistent, not one that has only been successful for one generation. Consistency is the key.

If you show your bitch, then you will already be familiar with several dogs and may have had a chance to discuss their suitability with their owners. You may even have seen various offspring of the dogs and seen what consistent stud dogs they are. Looking at the different dogs in the ring, see how they set about various tasks and observe their general dispositions. Then look up the breeding lines of the ones you like and after a while it will probably become evident that the common denominator of several of them will be a sire or even grandsire. Likewise, if a dog has a fault that stands out in your mind or a bad temperament, you might notice this too leads back to a particular sire. Be very cautious of studs which do have such dogs in their breeding!

A dog may appear aggressive due to his handler being aggressive or nervous. Therefore it is wise not to dismiss him on only one appearance; watch him over a period of time before reaching a conclusion. This is by far and away the most effective method of learning the traits of the dogs and their lines.

If you are purely a lay person, with no experience of the ring, then your job will be far more difficult. Where do you start? Well, initially, where did you purchase your bitch? If you bought her through a newspaper advertisement and your dog was bred by somebody like yourself, then you are practically back where you started, unless they used a reputable breeder for the dog. However, if you bought your dog from a reputable and well-known breeder you may refer back to them for advice on breeding your own bitch.

If you are still not sure about the credibility of breeders with stud dogs, ask The Kennel Club. They will send you a list of reputable breeders and breed clubs, who will advise you of highly regarded breeders from which to choose a suitable dog for your bitch.

Line Breeding

You may think that because you don't know enough about various 'lines' it will be safest to do an 'out-cross', which means to mate totally unrelated dogs. It is possible to double up on faults when line breeding by introducing a dog that appears in both the dog's and bitch's pedigree which might have a hereditary problem. Although you reduce this possibility by 'out-crossing', you also widen the gene pool of the puppies. By widening the gene pool you introduce so many different, unrelated dogs that it is impossible to know which will be the most dominant in reproducing his type and whether the puppies will develop sound characteristics.

Hybrid vigour is one result of out-crossing. The puppies will have strong, healthy constitutions, but will also possess characteristics you know nothing about, which could cause unpredictability and unsoundness of character. Line breeding enables you to foretell what characteristics are likely to be produced because you know the dogs in the pedigree.

The best way of line breeding is to mate into your bitch's pedigree without going to the dogs who are too closely related to her, e.g. father, brother, etc. A useful breeding pattern is to go back to the bitch's grandsire, but only if he is going to be worthy of being 'doubled up'.

It must be remembered that line breeding does not produce bad points or good points because they are already in the genes of that dog. What happens is that the genes that are in both dogs will be doubled up, be they good or bad. These genes could be brought out in an out-cross but they come out more quickly through line breeding.

The reason it is pointless to mate brother and sister is that you are not going forward. If you think about it, you are doubling up on the same faults and attributes and are not introducing a 'new' line at all. Only someone very knowledgeable about genetics would be able to mate a brother and sister to any good effect.

All breeds need prolific kennels with breeders who consistently produce puppies of their strain who carry 'type' as that kennel interprets it. One kennel might consistently produce the silver grey for which we all strive in Weimaraners through careful line breeding. Another kennel might always produce lovely hindquarters.

These kennels can be useful to those less knowledgeable about the intricacies of breeding. You can take your bitch to one of their studs and know to a certain extent what that line will give you in terms of colour, hindquarters or whatever. The breeder will know the attributes and faults of the dogs and can point out which of these are likely to reproduce in the puppies. Listen to his advice about what he would do and why.

It is not easy to have a number of dogs and make sure they all have the attention they need. A lot of time, energy and effort is expended by breeders of these kennels in order that the breed goes forward and is not left to stagnate or the quality deteriorate. If quality stock is produced by a kennel, then that stock will be successful in the field or ring, which is the best advertisement for the kennel and the breed. No caring breeder will knowingly breed faults into a breed he loves and wants to improve.

6 Mating, Pregnancy and Whelping

If you wish to mate your bitch, after much heart-searching, a number of other things should be taken into consideration. Choosing a suitable stud dog is top of the list. For genetic reasons this should be very carefully thought out, following the guidelines in Chapter 5.

Arranging for the Stud Dog

Always check that a stud dog is registered with The Kennel Club; if he is not then on no account use him. Pedigree dogs should be registered, and if they are not then you may have trouble registering the resulting litter until the sire's documents are sorted out by The Kennel Club.

Having made your choice of stud, you should discuss his availability with the owner. This should be done weeks before your bitch is due to come into season. That way you know you are both available at about that time and that the dog is not overbooked. It is also polite and considerate to book the use of a dog in this way and shows the owners that you are taking your responsibilities seriously. If, for whatever reason, the dates do not match, you may have to consider leaving your bitch until next season or choosing another dog.

Another reason to contact the stud owner early is to discuss stud fees. It is no good travelling to mate your bitch only to find that the fee is far more than you supposed. The only way to find out the cost is to ask the person charging the fee exactly what the terms and conditions are.

For instance, at our kennel if the bitch missed and didn't have a litter as expected, the owner would be entitled to a free return with a different bitch, or the same bitch using a different stud dog, all depending on the circumstances. We would never return the stud fee if a bitch missed, unless the dog proved to be sterile. We believe that when paying a stud fee, you are paying for the service not for a litter. Most breeders are of the same mind.

If your bitch is particularly lovely the stud owner may accept a puppy in lieu of payment, but this should be arranged before the mating takes place. If the bitch missed, you, the owner of the bitch, would not be required to pay a fee, unless provisions were made to the contrary, as the stud owner would have forfeited his fee by agreeing to take a puppy.

Payment in the form of fee or puppy is arranged before mating, not if and when the bitch whelps. It used to be that the stud fee equalled the price of a puppy, but now the price of a puppy generally far outways the stud fee. It used to be an accepted practice that an unproven male – one who had never sired a litter – was free. The general idea being that it would encourage somebody to prove the dog on their bitch. Nowadays, instead of this, there is an agreement for a pre-arranged fee to be paid only on the arrival of puppies. You should expect to have to pay a higher fee for the use of a mature or a Sh. Ch. dog. This is only fair when you consider that the progeny can be fairly assessed and will be more sought after if sired by a proven excellent dog.

If you are enquiring about the possible use of stud dogs, make sure that their owner knows that you are at present only considering their dogs for use. A stud owner will give you all the help you require so long as he is fully in the picture. No one likes being misled. If you set about this in the wrong way you will end up with no one allowing you to use his dog for stud.

Likewise it is imperative that the stud owner lays down his terms very clearly. If he does not consider the bitch worthy of breeding from, it is far kinder to say so. Also, the stud dog owner should make it clear if he expects all progeny to have their tails docked and dew claws removed. This should be clear before the mating and preferably written on the mating acceptance slip. If both sides make their intentions clear, it will make it a more enjoyable experience for all parties.

Using a dog at stud is not always as straightforward as nature would have you believe, although Weimaraners do tend to be sensible at stud as a rule. Always make sure that your chosen stud knows exactly what he is supposed to be doing. Do not allow a dog to simulate mating. It will not make him keener to mate bitches and will only confuse him. Don't scold him for riding bitches, call him away and make sure that he desists. Give him something more exciting to think about, or lift him off, talking cheerily to him, and play with him to divert him. If you beat him, he will jump off when he sees you coming, thinking he is about to get a good hiding, which won't help when you are trying to mate him.

A young dog will usually mate his first bitch at around nine months to a year in age if approached sensibly. If he is not ready don't goad him or you may well ruin him for life. If a young dog mating his first bitch fails to get her in whelp, don't worry.

Preparing the Bitch

Once everything is organised, you must wait for your bitch to come into season or on heat. About a month before she is due in season give her a good vitamin and mineral supplement and check that she is not over or under weight. This gives her the best possible chance of producing healthy eggs for fertilisation, conceiving and rearing a litter of healthy puppies. It is also wise to worm her. Make sure her booster vaccinations are up to date – check with the vet.

Be vigilant in looking for the signs of her impending season. It is no good ringing the stud owner to say you think she came into season on Monday, Tuesday or Wednesday. It has to be an accurate date to work out the best day for mating her.

Your bitch's vulva may swell before she starts bleeding but it is only when she first shows colour – bleeding – that it is counted as day one. The rule is that she should be mated between days eleven and fourteen, but everyone knows of an exception.

On day one ring the stud owner to discuss the course of action to be taken. There isn't a lot of use in travelling one hundred miles on a certain Saturday because it happens to be the day you have off work, if it isn't the day she needs to be mated.

Do not assume that if she is mated she will have puppies. If she is mated before she ovulates then the sperm may die before they have the chance to fertilise the eggs. If the mating is left too late, she might have ovulated and the eggs might have died before the sperm is able to reach them.

There are certain tell-tale signs to look for when a bitch is ready to be mated. If these are adhered to, you can usually guess the day she ovulates.

The swelling of the bitch's vulva may reduce and she will go 'out of colour', i.e. the discharge will become clear. However, I find that a lot of Weimaraner bitches can show colour throughout their season and yet conceive quite normally. Another sign is that if you scratch the base of her tail, she instinctively throws her tail up and to one side, a natural invitation to a dog to mate her. When she is really ready this reaction is instantaneous – she will stand still and arch her back in anticipation. Even a maiden, previously unmated bitch will show these signs, but often not as enthusiastically as a previously matched bitch. If in doubt discuss the matter with the stud dog owner; he should be able to advise you as to her reactions and the action necessary.

When she is ready it is your responsibility to take her to the dog. It is rare for the dog to visit the bitch, although this can be arranged if mutually acceptable. However, it is totally unacceptable to take a young dog to a strange place and expect him to perform. It could spoil his attitude to mating. Be aware that it is not advisable to ask for a mating to take place at a show. It is against Kennel Club rules for dogs to mate in the precinct of the showground. It is also unacceptable to take a bitch in season to a showground where dogs and bitches are shown together – usually at an Open Show. It is not too bad at Championship Shows because the dog classes are over before the bitches go into the ring. Always have a thought for people showing dogs and keep an in-season bitch well away until dog classes are over.

When you arrive ask if you may take your bitch somewhere to relieve herself. It is very uncomfortable for her when her instincts are urging her to mate if she has a full bladder.

Some owners of stud dogs take the bitch away to be mated, then invite you to witness the fact that the dog and bitch are tied. Bitches can be more responsive if their owners aren't watching.

In the natural state the bitch would choose her mate and flirt with him in her own territory. Indeed, if she managed to escape while in season, she would probably not come home until fully satisfied by, most likely, a very unsuitable local mongrel. We are in fact dictating an unnatural union.

The Mating Process

If an experienced dog is used, the bitch will enter the mating room and the dog will enter and immediately set about the business of mounting her. Obviously this can alarm the bitch and even her owner – another good reason for the owner not being present, unnerving the bitch. With a young dog make sure that you have someone you can trust, preferably a stranger to the bitch, standing by to hold her if you need him. Everyone is encouraged to be silent and a large audience is actively discouraged.

It is not wise for the owner of the bitch to hold her while she is being mated because they may sense each other's apprehension. As a breed Weimaraners can appear very virginal and sweet and shocked at the process. Even the sweetest natured bitch can turn into a demon and nip the dog. With the greatest respect, it is irrelevant how she feels, but if the stud is bitten it can spoil him for future matings.

If a bitch appears to be dry around the vulva, it may be due to her nervousness. Talk to her and calm her. The vulva can be lubricated with Vaseline which will enable the penis to penetrate easily. People may assume that the bitch is malformed internally and therefore the dog cannot penetrate her. This is rarely the case; it is usually inexperience on the part of the handlers that is causing the problem.

A bitch who appears nervous and reluctant or dry will often settle after the dog has tried to mount her a couple of times. The dog will often flirt with her, nestling in her ears as if to whisper reassurances.

It is amazing how often a bitch will instinctively throw her tail, even when mentally she gives every appearance of wanting nothing to do with the whole process. Her body is ready to be mated even if her brain hasn't quite accepted the idea of it. Often you will find that if you return for a second mating after forty-eight hours the bitch invariably rushes into the mating quarters, tail wagging for a second go!

It is possible for an experienced handler with an experienced stud dog to mate a bitch who isn't quite ready. It isn't advisable though, even it if would make you happy. Far better to come back in a couple of days when the timing is perfect. A lot of people bring their bitch too early on, simply because they are nervous about missing the right time. Don't waste everybody's time, relax and be objective.

There are stud owners who agree to the dogs playing for an hour or so before mating to familiarise themselves with each other. However, by the time the bitch is eager to be mounted, the dog may be thoroughly worn out and have lost interest in mating her. Many people rapidly lose their high ideals after such an occurrence, especially if they have travelled a hundred miles for the mating to take place.

People often ask for a second mating as a form of insurance. Some breeders advise only one mating, but if the dogs were in the wild they would be mating at every opportunity during the season, when the bitch is receptive. The dogs generally are not mated on consecutive days, because if the bitch ovulates on the day after mating the sperm will still be alive to fertilise the eggs. Mating for a second time two days later gives you four days' leeway for fertilisation rather than two. We often only mate once if we feel the bitch was right and the mating went well. There is no truth in thinking that the more times you mate, the more puppies you will have.

Let the bitch flirt as much as possible to excite the dog and quietly encourage him, telling him how good he is. If he is slow to become involved, hold the bitch under the gut, scratching her back so that she stands square and solid, ready for the dog. Encourage the dog all the time, then when he mounts quietly back off so that he doesn't feel threatened. Don't move right away though, as generally he will feel happier and more confident with you close to him. There may come a time if a bitch is nasty when you have to hold her tight, and if he won't mate a bitch with you there all sorts of problems can ensue.

When the dog begins to work, hold the bitch's vulva, guiding it towards the dog's penis. Don't touch the dog. When he enters the bitch, hang on to her so that she doesn't move, making sure that everything goes as smoothly as possible.

The Tie

If you have never been present at the mating of dogs before, you may not know that they tie. The dog mounts the bitch and works; when he penetrates he will hang on to the bitch round her waist and work harder. After a while he will become quiet and still and he will lift his front legs off

the bitch, turning himself. They are then tied together. He will usually lift his hind leg over the bitch and they will stand quietly back to back.

A young dog can look a little confused when he ties for the first time. Don't rush to turn him, but stroke him gently, reassuring him and letting him decide when to turn. Young dogs often lift their front legs to one side and do not turn fully for a while. Leave it up to him, it will help him gain confidence.

If the bitch has had to be muzzled for any reason, then you may remove it at this time. It is very unlikely that a Weimaraner bitch will show aggression once the tie has occurred. She usually stands quietly and sensibly, sometimes moaning and slavering.

Just why the tie occurs is open to speculation. Unlike a cow or horse that has one egg to fertilise, the bitch has a number of eggs. My theory is that while the dogs are tied the sperm have more chance of fertilising all available eggs; the male pumps prostatic secretion fluid while tied which helps the sperm reach the eggs for fertilisation.

Not every mating results in a tie but this is unusual. I have known bitches wriggle at the wrong moment when the dog has not been penetrating deeply

This shows a dog and bitch 'tied'. Notice a soft nylon lead on the bitch, which can be used to restrain her from snapping at the male.

enough to tie. However, if he is held in the bitch for a minute or two while he ejaculates, fertilisation can and does occur. Don't be tempted to use another dog if this happens in your case.

When the dog and bitch are mating, the penis extends into the vulva. At the body end of the penis two bulbs swell up inside the bitch and are held by her, making the tie possible. It is said that the bitch determines the length of tie. However, having spent many hours in the mating quarters I have come to the conclusion that although the bitch holds the penis in her with her muscles the tie actually ends when the dog's bulbs start to reduce, informing the bitch when to relax.

The tie can last for any time from two minutes to more than an hour; usually it lasts about twenty minutes. Each dog tends to tie for the same length of time regardless of the bitch he is mating. A young dog tends to tie for only a few minutes. However, as he settles into his work, his length of tie will stabilise. The length of tie is not relevant to the size of the litter. If I had to choose a dog of ours that generally produced the largest litter, I would say that the one with the shortest tie had the edge.

Hold the bitch firmly until the dog turns. After the tie, keep hold of the lead or under her gut to stop her from jumping about or trying to sit down, but don't hang on to her head tightly. The tighter you hold on, the more unsettled and restricted she will feel, and she will try to pull away. It is wise to stay with the pair at this time. Sometimes it is necessary to hold the bitch around the gut to stop her sinking down. A gentle word to both animals is all that is needed to reassure them.

Once a tie is effected, never try to hurry the procedure. Even if a mismatch has occurred with a mongrel, wait patiently until they part and then take your bitch to the vet for the requisite treatment. An injection can be administered to prevent her from holding in whelp, but do not on any account rely on it as a regular treatment. These high doses of hormones should be used once or twice in a lifetime, if at all, due to the high risks involved. It is far wiser to consider the other options open to you and to watch your bitch more carefully when she is in season.

Once the tie is over, less dominant males in the pack may sneak in to mate the bitch. If the tie didn't occur males presumably could and would mate at will. In the wild they would turn back to back naturally, and would therefore be more able to ward off predators and inquisitive pack members.

When the tie is completed the pair will part naturally. Both dogs are let loose in the mating quarters to tidy themselves up. The dog may wish to tidy the bitch and this is quite natural and acceptable behaviour. Let the dog play with the bitch. He won't instantly mate her again, but if you let him flirt you will see his confidence grow.

Old wives' tales abound about what happens next: If the dog licks the bitch, it means she will conceive. If the bitch urinates it will wash out the sperm before fertilisation can occur. The bitch should not be allowed to sit down for ten minutes. The bitch's hindquarters should be lifted up and shaken slightly to ensure the sperm gets into the uterus so conception can take place.

There is no truth in any of these sayings, although it has to be said that a few eminent dog people, not normally prone to fanciful ways, do adhere to them. Don't be alarmed if the stud owner lifts up your bitch; it may not do any good but it won't harm her.

It is also the practice of some to wash the dog down in a mild antiseptic solution after mating. I prefer to leave well alone; it may be the case that the more you interfere the more risk of infection you create.

Mating is a fundamental exercise for all life and should be fairly trouble free. Your attitude helps: you have to inspire confidence in the dog, direct him without being dominant, convince him he is six feet tall and tell him how clever he is for being about to achieve this wonderful act. If he has never been bitten by a bitch under any circumstances when mating, and you ensure this does not happen in the future, then you are well on the way to having a successful stud dog. Each animal is different, you just have to learn his idiosyncrasies.

The Mating Quarters

I keep referring to the mating quarters, because it is best to choose a specific place for mating and to use it every time. You won't confuse your dogs, because they will know that if they are asked to go there they are expected to perform. It also means that they are conditioned to mate only in that place, so that if anyone visits with a Weimaraner bitch, the dogs don't expect to mate her and won't jump all over her.

A stable can be used as the mating quarters and should be private, noise-free and free from other distractions. Cover the floor in straw so that it is even and not slippery. It is very frustrating trying to mate dogs on a slippery floor, and the dog does not take kindly to being followed about with a mat. The garden is fine in summer, but what happens when it is raining or blowing a gale?

After the Mating

If the bitch misses, especially a maiden, it may well be wise for the vet to test her for infection before she is mated again. It is also possible to have her swabbed daily by the vet when in season. This will tell you when she ovulates. The only disadvantage in doing this is that you will receive the results daily. Therefore, when you receive the news of ovulation you must travel speedily to the stud. This may prove difficult if the chosen stud lives several hundred miles away.

After the mating is finished and everybody is presentable again, put the bitch back in the car, out of the way of any other marauding male. The dog is put back in his run. We don't have the problem of our dogs fighting after one has mated a bitch, but be wary as the possibility is always there. The dog that has been used might feel full of himself and a bit cocky and the other dogs may well be jealous. Tempers could then be raised.

Even if he is the only male, he may receive attention from his curious female companions, which may unnerve him and make him act out of character. It may be best to leave him on his own for a while, to give him time to settle himself down again.

After the mating you will receive from the stud dog owner a copy pedigree of the dog used, a receipt for the stud fee, giving the date of mating and whelping, and usually the green form. This is The Kennel Club document needed to register the litter and requires the dog owner's signature as well as the bitch owner's signature. If neither of you has this form it can be applied for when you have the litter. If you pay the stud fee by cheque, then the stud owner may well wait for the cheque to clear before he signs the form. Having completed all the formalities you then go home and wait.

The Bitch in Whelp

Every bitch handles pregnancy differently, some show distinct signs that they are in whelp. These signs can be more difficult to read with a maiden bitch. Others can fool you.

A number of bitches in whelp seem to absorb the puppies at a later date, which does happen, but not, I feel, as often as is supposed. In many cases the bitch is probably having a false pregnancy.

Between three and four weeks into the pregnancy your vet, or an experienced breeder, can manipulate the bitch's abdomen and feel the puppies. They feel like small golf balls, but they disappear again after four weeks, so you have to be swift and accurate to detect them. No self-respecting vet will say definitely one way or the other, but he will offer an opinion. However, a good and experienced vet is generally correct in his supposition. These days your vet can ultra-sonically scan your bitch.

Most breeders have their own signs to look for in a pregnant bitch and some of these are: the very front teats will grow and become pink; the bitch goes off her food three weeks after mating; the bitch's habits totally change. My own is that the backbone becomes prominent and the bitch thickens in the waist, but she does not necessarily fatten over the ribs.

Usually by six weeks you will know if the bitch is in whelp and by seven weeks it can be generally confirmed by the eye, unless she is having only one or two or in other extreme cases.

The bitch should have a mineral and vitamin supplement and calcium throughout her pregnancy. If you are not sure what she needs, ask your vet's advice. The general feeling is that it is best not to interfere too much. Just make sure she has a good quality diet.

As the pregnancy advances she may require more food that normal. If she becomes very heavy, but thin over the backbone and ribs, she is probably having a large litter. Make sure she has adequate food to cover all their needs. If, on the other hand, she is fat and bonny all over, don't overfeed her as this will do her no good when she whelps.

Your bitch should have been wormed before she was mated, but if parasites are suspected worm her during the pregnancy on the vet's advice.

It is often a good idea to give the bitch a drink of milk during the last couple of weeks of her pregnancy. Try to avoid lots of drinks last thing at night. As the puppies grow pressure is put on the bladder, making it difficult for a normally clean bitch to last through the night. She may try to wake you up during the night or you may find a puddle on the kitchen floor. Don't be too hard on her under these circumstances – once she has whelped she will revert to her normal clean self.

In the last week of parturition, the puppies can be seen moving, particularly when the bitch lies on her side. With the short-coated Weimaraner they are especially obvious. You may find your bitch's abdomen becoming the main attraction of an evening, not the television.

The gestation period is sixty-three days, although a bitch can go a week over with no ill effects. However, after a couple of days over the due date, ring your vet and ask his advice. We have found that a maiden bitch can be three days early, and we had one litter a full week early with no ill effects.

The Whelping Box

You should prepare the whelping area well in advance of the due date. We have a special whelping kennel that is scalded, disinfected and cleaned several times before and after each litter of puppies. The kennel is used only by whelping bitches.

The kennel has a whelping box and about a fortnight before she is due, the bitch is put in the kennel to sleep. This gives her time to become comfortable in her new quarters and allows for any unexpected early arrivals. When the bitch is due we bring the whelping box into the house and put it in a quiet corner and fix a heat lamp above it. The bitch sleeps in the house until after her delivery.

The whelping box measures 35 in x 40 in x 5 in with a 4 in lip turning in on the box. If the box is too large, the bitch can become distressed if the puppies move to the outer corners. If it is too small, then the bitch may accidentally squash a puppy or two. The lip helps prevent this happening as the bitch cannot lie right up to the side of the box. Weimaraners are, on the whole, sensible mothers and try not to damage their puppies. The walls of your box may need to be higher to prevent older puppies escaping. It is also possible to have a rail fitted to the box. It is very important to have either a lip or a rail on the whelping box.

Newborn puppies require heat in both summer and winter. They need a constant heat of 75°F or 24°C. A heat lamp can be placed over the box so no wires are left dangling to be chewed, and the lamp can be lowered or lifted as needed. It also provides a focal point for the puppies. If it is too warm, the puppies will head away from it and if it is not warm enough, they will huddle on top of each other under it, shivering. Make sure there are no draughts near the whelping box as they cause as many problems as cold and damp conditions.

There is always the chance that a bitch will take you completely by surprise and whelp in an unarranged place at her own convenience. You may find her only after the puppies are cold and beginning to suffer. The first thing to do is to warm the puppies. The fastest and safest way of doing it is to fill a washing up bowl with hand hot water – blood heat – and hold the puppies in it. They should be immersed totally, up to their heads. This will quickly bring their temperature back up to the required heat. Then dry the puppies well with a towel and keep them warm. If you are still worried about the litter, consult your vet.

Newspapers are invaluable at this time. We cover the box in newspaper and then cover the newspaper with Vetbed. Newspaper absorbs any liquid and can be burned after use, so it will not harbour germs.

Vetbed is particularly useful during whelping. It allows moisture to pass through, leaving the bedding dry and warm. The puppies can grip it, so they don't scrabble around with splayed legs when they try to feed. It is easily washed and dried, so it is hygienic. The bitches lie on it happily, without scratching it into a ball as they do with a blanket. If the bedding is scratched up puppies can be lost in the bed and inadvertently squashed.

Whelping

The bitch normally goes off her food the day prior to whelping. Having said that, our Weimaraner bitches eat between whelps. She will start digging and show signs of wanting to whelp in a certain place, often on top of your bed. Remember Weimaraners are a determined breed: a stern command directing her back to the whelping box is often needed. She needs convincing that the whelping box is the only place to be.

As labour progresses, the bitch will need to relieve herself often. She will also start to pant and dither about; this is normal and can last a day or so with nothing to worry about. Her temperature may drop from 101.5°F to about 98°F (38.5–36.5°C).

As the bitch becomes imminent, you will see her stomach contracting and she will start to push. The water sac of that puppy may burst at this time. The birth should follow fairly quickly after she starts pushing.

If nothing has happened after half an hour take her for a walk around the garden to see if that speeds things up. If you go during the night, take a torch and watch her very carefully. If this does not have the required result, have a word with your vet. He may advise taking her to the surgery. The car journey may well stir things up and on arrival you may have a puppy and a red face, or your bitch may require a caesarian section, in which case she needs to be in the surgery anyway. The puppy might be lying at an angle to the birth canal and your vet may be able to turn it so it can be delivered normally. An experienced breeder may be able to do this too, but a novice must never attempt to interfere in such a way – leave it to the experts.

There is no set pattern or time between whelps. They can follow each other quickly or, as with one of our bitches, it can take twenty-four hours to whelp four puppies, with ten hours between the last two. This is an extreme case and normally a bitch should not be left longer than about three hours between whelps. If you suspect any distress or anything untoward, consult your vet immediately.

Each whelp has its own water sac and afterbirth, although you will not necessarily see either of these. If the bitch is very fastidious in her delivery procedure, she may eat the afterbirth as soon as the whelp is delivered, making it impossible for you to distinguish between her enthusiasm for cleaning the whelp and eating the afterbirth. I saw my first placenta only after many deliveries.

Puppies are born as most mammals are, head first. If they come backwards, there is no real problem, so long as they are born relatively quickly. In this case the placenta may break before delivery due to the extra stress put on it and the puppy has to be delivered quickly or it may suffocate.

The need to help a puppy out of the birth canal may arise, although this is a very rare occurrence. Be very gentle and don't on any account rush or panic. Hold the puppy as firmly as possible around the body if possible. Pull gently with the contractions and ease the puppy out with your finger gently stretching the vulva.

The bitch may well wish to relieve herself between whelps. This is fine so long as she is watched carefully. I have heard of a novice letting her bitch out in the garden after whelping eight pups. The next day she found two dead puppies in the garden, a most distressing and dissatisfactory find.

One reads of all sorts of implements one should have ready for the birth. I firmly believe that you should oversee the birth, but not interfere unless forced. You can usually do more harm than good when interfering without just cause.

As the first pup is born, the bitch will lick herself insistently, pausing to push; she may grumble or moan as the pup is born. One of our bitches, obviously shocked by the pain of the labour, turned to grab at the puppy being delivered. I restrained her head, so she didn't inadvertently damage the puppy. On completion of the birth I released her head and she broke the water sac as normal, with no thought of hurting her baby.

After the Birth

Immediately after the birth, the bitch will take the umbilical cord in her back teeth and cut through it: this severs the puppy from his mother. She will lick him vigorously, possibly rolling him over quite roughly. Don't be alarmed as this is what he needs to stimulate his heart, lungs and circulation. It is wonderful how she seems to know instinctively just what he needs.

If for some reason she doesn't chew through the cord, then you must do it, but not with your scissors. You should sever the cord with your thumb nail, making sure that it is not pulled and torn from the body. About an inch of cord should be left attached to the pup. If you do this job with scissors, you are effectively leaving a sharp, clean opening for bacteria. Severing the cord with your nails or the bitch's teeth leaves a jagged edge which heals faster, reducing the risk of infection.

If the bitch is feeling poorly and tired, and is not up to licking the puppy, rub him roughly up and down his back to stimulate him into action. If he has had a difficult birth, gently massage his heart after clearing the mucus from his face, especially from his nose and mouth. Don't rush to do these jobs though; it is far better for the mother to do them herself. She is far more proficient at them and performing them aids the bonding procedure between mother and pup.

A new mother may go overboard with her first baby and it is often a relief for all when the second one arrives to divert her attention a little.

I like to make sure that the puppy suckles after he has been cleaned by his mother. Weimaraner puppies generally shuffle round to the teats and suck heartily. Other breeds do not always show the same determination at such an early age.

The colostrum produced immediately after birth provides initial protection against disease. This early suckling also stimulates milk production in the dam. The more suckling and demand for milk, the more she will produce and vice versa. Unless there is something dramatically wrong with the bitch and she requires veterinary attention, she will generally produce enough milk for her litter. Don't assume that just because her mammary glands are not swinging on the ground and dripping with milk, she isn't producing enough for all the litter needs; she probably is.

You do have to watch for Mastitis, an inflammation of the milk glands, during the days following whelping. If the mammary glands become red, swollen and hard, then try to expel milk from the teat and encourage a strong puppy to suckle from it. This may be painful for her, but if done early enough it may prevent a serious attack that will need treatment. However, if this doesn't work consult your vet, who will treat it with antibiotics. It is usually best to try to avoid the use of antibiotics administered to the bitch as much as possible, because they are passed from mother to puppies, who in turn might develop an immunity to them. Prevention is best, so be vigilant. If the Mastitis is left untreated, a serious infection will develop.

The bitch's motions may be loose and black for a day or two, but this should quickly revert to normal and is usually the result of the bitch devouring the afterbirths. During and just after whelping a green discharge may be evident, but don't be alarmed because this is quite normal. After whelping, a clear red vaginal discharge is evident, persisting for a week or more. Providing it remains fresh and does not have a foul odour there is no need to be concerned.

However, if the discharge becomes dark and the bitch shows signs of lethargy, thirst and loss of appetite, she may have an infection. Don't hesitate to contact your vet about it. The infection may be Metritis, which is an inflammation of the uterus, caused by a retained afterbirth or even in extreme cases a retained, dead puppy. The temperature of the bitch will rise and the discharge will probably smell revolting. This infection may well affect the lactation of the bitch, so it is imperative that she receives treatment immediately.

If in any doubt as to when she is finished whelping, consult your vet; he will be able to ascertain if she has finished or not. He may consider giving her an injection to contract her uterus to expel any afterbirth or remaining puppies. He may even inject her with antibiotics to safeguard against possible infection. An experienced breeder will probably know by instinct when the bitch has finished and if everything is in order. If all is well, the bitch settles and rests easily, or may even sleep with her new family suckling. It is a grand sight!

The day after whelping, you will find your bitch rests contentedly. She may not be too willing to pay a call outside, so you may have to take her. Be careful if you have to put a lead on her to force her out, as she may tread on an unwary puppy in the process. It is unlikely that she will tread on puppies in the normal course of events, and only when being forced to move against her wishes.

On the completion of parturition. Notice the stripes on the puppies.

Encourage her to drink a lot. Anything is suitable, water, milk, egg and milk, even cocoa if so desired: all will help her milk supply. Her consumption of solid food will return when she is fit and ready. Encourage her with a titbit if you must but, being a Weimaraner, she will soon sense her advantage and use it.

If there are other dogs or bitches in the vicinity, watch they don't intrude on her. All her instincts and protectiveness are heightened and she may snarl and snap at them for this reason. Have humans, particularly children, show her the same respect. We have found that canines are as interested as any humans in the size and health of a new litter. The males particularly find the puppies fascinating and will sneak in to peep if not watched carefully.

Before, during and after the birth everybody should keep a low profile. The bitch will not want to be pestered by dogs or people. It will only serve to worry her and she may begin to fret. If thoroughly disturbed, she may try to move the litter. You and a good book will be quite sufficient company for her.

Culling Litters

There are varying views about the possible culling of large litters. The breed masters in Germany dictated that large litters must be culled to six puppies. This was later raised to seven.

Personally I feel that if puppies are fit and healthy they should live. However, if a puppy is born with a cleft palate, an abnormality or an obvious deviation from the Standard of the Weimaraner which will impair the puppy's chance of enjoying a full, normal and happy life, I would not hesitate in having that puppy put to sleep humanely by my vet.

Some people believe that mis-marked puppies should also be destroyed. These ginger markings are obviously a throwback to the Weimaraner's ancestors and appear around the muzzle, below the knee and hocks of the legs and under the tail. They are rather like the markings of a Dobermann. Others may appear to have ginger markings on the eyebrow when moulting, which disappear again afterwards. Although the dog is usually sound and fit, and therefore able to lead a normal life, these markings are a grave fault and the dog should never be bred from. I hate to see them, but on the condition that the animal is sterilised, I would let the puppy live and be homed as a pet without papers.

Even with a large litter in mind, I would let nature take its course on the subject of culling. If one puppy suffers from always being last to a teat, hook him on to one every time you pass the whelping box. If he lives all well and good, but if he dies it was just not meant to be. Do not be too quick to think of supplementing a weakling. We have only supplemented a puppy once and in the end it turned out the puppy had a congenital abnormality and had to be put to sleep when he was three weeks old.

Care of the Mother

Rearing a litter of ten or twelve puppies does take a lot out of a bitch, but in my experience it does not have a more adverse effect than rearing a small litter, providing that she has the best possible care.

The bitch should have had her supplements while in whelp and they should be continued while she is nursing. A high-protein diet should be fed twice or thrice daily, as well as a milk feed. All of this should keep her brimming with health.

Some bitches put everything into their puppies, leaving themselves looking extremely poorly. Once she has stopped nursing, she will quickly regain her body weight. Although it is distressing to see a bitch in such an emaciated state, it is nice to know the puppies are receiving the best possible nourishment at this important first stage of their life. Other bitches rear a thriving litter with absolutely no loss of condition to themselves.

Immediately after whelping and for the following three days, keep a close watch on your bitch for signs of Eclampsia or 'milk fever'. Eclampsia is caused by a sudden drop in blood calcium, which might be due to the bitch having to provide a sudden rush of milk for the newborn litter, or she might be undernourished. Make sure you keep up the calcium supply.

The initial signs are that the bitch becomes restless, perhaps even apprehensive, and the litter may become restless. If left untreated, the bitch may collapse and have convulsions. It is a very acute condition and veterinary treatment should be sought immediately or the bitch may well die. The vet will inject calcium directly into her bloodstream and this will effect a seemingly miraculous recovery. Watch her carefully though throughout her lactation as it may recur.

Hand-rearing the Puppies

If the mother dies for this or any other reason and you have to hand-rear a litter, it can be done successfully, but have as many helpers as possible, as the puppies will initially need feeding every two hours. If a foster mother can be found, it could be the best solution, though you must take care that she doesn't reject strange puppies.

If you do have to do it yourself, make sure that you use a bitch milk substitute. Cow's milk, evaporated milk, etc., are not suitable and must not be used. They are of totally the wrong nutritional value and do more harm than good.

Always follow manufacturers' instructions carefully when making up the puppy milk. It is finely balanced to provide exactly the right nutrients in the right quantity for your puppies. As with human babies, newborn puppies benefit from consistency in their food and any deviations can cause gastric problems.

A weak puppy may need feeding by hand with a syringe, obviously without the needle in place. It is far better, however, to use a specially designed bottle and teat for rearing small animals. This way the puppy gets to suckle, which is an important part of his comfort and care. Don't hold the puppies, but do try to emulate their mother as much as possible.

If the litter was orphaned at birth and never received the mother's colostrum, you have to be very careful about infection. The puppies will be far more vulnerable to disease than a litter suckling their mother's milk. Visitors should be discouraged and you will have to be extra vigilant about cleanliness. Your vet should advise you about the benefits of vaccinating such a litter earlier than usual.

The mother cleans and stimulates the litter into passing urine and faeces. She does this by licking the genital area of each puppy. You can use damp, clean cotton wool, as fingers can introduce infection. A good time to do this is after feeds, when you wash their hands and faces.

Hand-reared puppies are usually more ready to lap at their food, which initially has the consistency of porridge, because they are not as settled and food dominates their life. Puppies nurtured by their mother can snuggle up to her and they are contented and relaxed.

Puppies that are thriving are fat and contented. They lie quietly, only seeming to move when they go to suckle. When asleep a contented puppy twitches, as though dreaming, and does not make a lot of noise.

The Growing Puppy

Weimaraner puppies are striped at birth. The stripes are a sign of good health, but gradually disappear over a period of a week or so. There is no need to panic, your bitch hasn't mis-mated with the local tiger!

During the first three weeks, the litter will need little from you. They will eat, sleep and grow under the loving attention of their mother. You need to worry only if you find the puppies scrawny, very active and piling up in a heap to sleep. These are signs of malnutrition or that the puppies are cold. If your bitch is short of milk, consult your vet; don't hang about because attention is needed fast.

Occasionally newborn whelps need to have their nails cut, but more often this is done when they are a week old. It is a very easy procedure, which can be carried out with ordinary bathroom clippers. The nails are transparent, therefore one can easily see how short to cut them.

It is imperative that nails are kept short, otherwise the mother can become very sore. Puppies use their front legs to pommel the mammary gland when suckling to help stimulate the supply of milk.

Docked Tails and Dew Claws

Tails are docked and dew claws are removed between the age of three and five days. Everyone has their own, very definite opinion about the docking of dogs' tails. However, it is a simple procedure, which causes very little pain if done properly.

If you look at the Weimaraner puppy's tail, you will see the natural docking point. However, a good gauge for your vet is for him to hold a ten pence coin under the tail, close to the body; he will then dock at the joint below the ten pence. Potassium Permanganate crystals are quickly applied with damp cotton wool to reduce the risk of bleeding and infection.

The dew claws are removed with curved blade scissors, which hook and snip at the same time. This leaves as small a wound as possible. Again they should be treated with Potassium Permanganate crystals.

The whole process is quick and simple and the puppies often squeal more at being picked up than at the actual operation, if it is done properly. Puppy number four is usually snuggled up and asleep with the litter by the time number five is returned after docking, so I don't think it causes too much

The natural docking point.

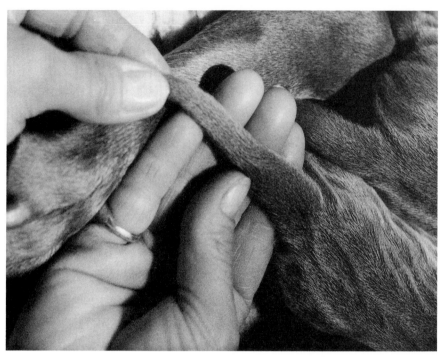

stress. The bitch should be taken away and distracted though, as she may well become distressed.

Why do we dock?

Weimaraners are an active, athletic and brave breed, who when working or even out for a walk will go in any cover after scent. Therefore, be it dense cover, barbed wire, coarse bush, etc., their solid, finely-coated body will become scratched and their long lashing tail could and will often be lacerated in such conditions.

It is very difficult to keep a damaged tail still while it heals. Therefore amputation often becomes the only option. This has to be done under anaesthetic and is not the simple operation that docking a puppy is. If docking saves one adult dog in fifty having to have his tail amputated, then it is justified in my opinion.

Three Weeks

The eyes open between ten days and two weeks after the puppies are born. They start at the corners and gradually open over a few days. Sometimes pus can weep from newly opening eyes. If this happens, bathe the eye with a boiled and cooled saline solution as often as necessary to keep the eyes clear of pus. If the eyes haven't cleared by the time they are fully open, have your vet look at them. The pups start to focus properly at about three weeks. They start to hear when they are about two to three weeks old. The litter becomes really interesting after three weeks.

Food   Food can be introduced for the first time at three to three and a half weeks. Each litter is different; some will accept it more readily than others. The first meal we offer is rice pudding. The puppies are placed around a shallow dish and, once they get the flavour, are often in it, feet and all. Mum enjoys clearing up afterwards.

After a couple of feeds of this, we introduce a leading brand of canned puppy meat, mushed up with a drop of boiled water. The puppies usually love this different flavour. Give this meal at dinner time. The bitch should be away from the puppies, perhaps out on a walk, and only after they have finished should she be allowed back. She cleans up the dish and the puppies and then the puppies settle down for a drink.

A lot of people prefer to feed scraped beef or mince. I stick to the tinned variety of puppy meat as I know it contains all the supplements in the right quantity that a growing puppy needs. It is finely balanced and I am not sure that the same can be said of meat alone.

Worming   At three to three and a half weeks the puppies should be wormed for the first time. Remember to worm mum as well, as she cleans up after the puppies. A wormer in tablet form is the easiest to administer.

The mouth of the puppy is held open with the thumb and finger of one hand while the other hand puts the tablet down the back of the throat. Be firm and gentle and it should all be completed with the minimum of fuss. If you don't put the tablet down the throat far enough, the puppy may be able to spit it out. You may not realise that he has spit it out and the puppy will be left unwormed.

Licking his lips on his release is usually a good sign that a dog has swallowed the tablet. If he doesn't, then more often than not he has it hidden in his mouth somewhere. If worms are spotted in the motions of the puppy, pick them up and burn them.

Worming should continue every fortnight until the puppy goes to his new home. The new owners must be advised of your worming procedure and told to seek their vet's advice about further worming. He will know if disease is prevalent in his area, and may advise vaccinations at an earlier time than usual.

Four Weeks

By four weeks, the puppies are brimming with health and looking more like

Five-week-old puppies. Shredded paper bedding and shavings are used in the playing area, because they are easily cleaned out when fouling occurs and are sweet smelling.

little dogs. Their navy blue eyes are becoming brighter, their ears longer and their teeth are coming through like sharp needles. Don't forget to keep trimming their nails, which are also like needles.

The mother will be more willing to spend time away from the litter. She may also start to regurgitate food. This is an instinct left over from the wild.

Before the dog was domesticated, this would have been the first solid food the puppies were introduced to, so don't rush your bitch to the vet, thinking that something is seriously wrong. Nowadays we feed the puppies their first solid food.

Some bitches will stop clearing up after their puppies as they take more and more solid food. They clear up after them from birth, so for the first three weeks you may not notice any mess or smell. As the puppies are now very active and parting with waste at every opportunity, it will be well nigh impossible to keep the Vetbed clean and sweet. It is probably best to bed the puppies on shredded paper from now on. This can be purchased in large plastic-covered bales and is very hygienic. Wood shavings can be put outside the whelping box to keep the kennel clean and sweet.

Newspaper is an alternative, but it is a never-ending task clearing it away and it does not have the clean, fresh aroma of wood shavings. Shavings are easily shovelled up and disposed of, whereas the alternatives are not as easily disposed of because they are more bulky.

The puppies should be on four feeds a day. Weetabix and milk should be fed for breakfast. Remember to use a bitch milk substitute, or goat's milk, and include any dietary supplements at this feed, which is readily taken because the puppies are hungriest then. You won't forget to add the supplements if you make a habit of including them at this meal every day.

After breakfast is over and dirty bedding changed, the bitch should be let back in to feed the puppies. She should be removed in the late morning.

Lunchtime should consist of the meat meal. Again the mother should be let in to clean up and give the pups a drink. Tea follows the same pattern. Supper should be about ten o'clock and then the bitch should be left to sleep with the litter.

Weaning the Puppies

After five weeks the puppies are quite rough with their mother and she is best left with them for only short intervals throughout the day. By six weeks the puppies have piercing blue eyes, which are capable of melting the hardest heart. They are cheeky and will play happily. As soon as they hear your voice, their tummies rumble and they rush to their food dishes. They will be consuming large amounts of food. Give them enough to fill them, but don't overfeed them as this may turn them into picky eaters.

At five to six weeks of age we begin to reduce the time the bitch spends with the puppies, gradually weaning them from their mother. The demand on the mother for milk will gradually be reduced, allowing lactation to cease naturally. Eventually you should miss a day of putting her with the pups to complete the drying-out process.

Keep feeling her mammary glands to make sure individual teats are not becoming hard and swollen. If she is uneven in drying up, allow a puppy to suckle the full teat and keep checking.

By six and a half weeks the puppies should be weaned. This benefits the puppies and their mother. The work of getting the bitch back into tip-top condition then starts. Long walks, preferably uphill, and swimming will soon get her undercarriage up neatly.

If the weather permits, puppies can be allowed out to play for short periods. Our adult dogs play happily with puppies on warm sunny days. Don't leave them out for too long, as they tire quickly and soon catch a chill. Young puppies don't have the experience or knowledge that tells them to go back inside where it is warm, they just lie down, curl up and shiver. Be careful if allowing older dogs to play with the puppies; they must be disease-free and fully vaccinated, otherwise they might be harbouring something that could be transmitted to the puppies.

Do not allow the older dogs to be too rough with the youngsters or to nip them. It is wise to remember that puppies head straight for every canine undercarriage, regardless of sex, and adults, particularly males, are not too happy about this.

Selling the Puppies

How, where and when do you sell puppies having bred them?

Make sure you work out the logistics of finding them good homes before you breed a litter. A reputable and well-known breeder is often willing to offer help and advice. Generally the stud owner should show responsibility for a litter by his dog and he should wish to contribute to the litter's well being.

After the birth of the litter, ensure that they are all hale and hearty. Then after a couple of days inform the people wishing to purchase a pup that they are welcome to come and view them. Do not accept promises or deposits beforehand in case the prospective owners or the puppies don't materialise. It is wise that they leave a deposit for the puppy after the visit when they have had a chance to reconsider the pros and cons of owning a Weimaraner. The deposit ensures that you are happy that they definitely want a puppy and that they are suitable owners, and they are happy that one is reserved for them.

If there are puppies remaining unsold at three weeks, you should consider the prospect of advertising them. By doing this early, you have the opportunity to vet potential buyers and weed out unsuitable applicants. Your judgement will not then be clouded by the need to find homes for eight-week-old puppies.

It is unwise for a buyer to visit the litter at eight weeks and immediately take a puppy home. They should go home and consider the matter carefully before making that commitment. They also have time to prepare properly for his arrival.

Where to Advertise

The best way to advertise is through the breed clubs. The clubs have rules which have to be complied with. Therefore if the member behaves in a way that is detrimental to the breed, that person won't be allowed to retain his membership to the club. Consequently the breed club puppy list should contain reputable breeders from the breed's point of view. If someone has bothered to find out about the club, his intentions are most likely honourable regarding the breed.

You may wish to advertise through the country press or the canine publications. Again the people reading such publications will not be ringing on a whim. The local rag should be your very last resort. Many look through the dog-for-sale section out of boredom, see an unusual sounding breed, like the Weimaraner, and ring up to arrange a visit. They invariably never turn up or appear out of curiosity with no serious interest in the breed at all.

When your puppies leave you the new owner should be given the following:

Registration certificate from the Kennel Club (this can be forwarded if necessary)
Diet sheet
Previous worming particulars
Pedigree
Receipt and condition of sale (e.g. that you will accept the return of the puppy if need be).

In your enthusiasm for your puppies do not make claims that might not stand up to scrutiny, such as they are show puppies and will win, they will be perfectly behaved or they will never bite. Remember, NEVER say never.

Code of Conduct

The Weimaraner Club of Great Britain have produced a code of conduct that should be read by prospective members of the club.

1 Members will consider the welfare of their dogs and the breed above any personal gain or profit and will take any responsibility for any dogs they own.

2 Members will only breed from Weimaraners of sound temperament, which show natural ability and will always strive to produce Weimaraners conforming to the Standard as published by The Kennel Club.

3 Members will not allow their stud dogs to serve bitches of less than two years or over the age of seven. Neither dogs nor bitches in poor health, of unsound temperament or with any serious hereditary faults will be used for breeding.

4 Stud dog owners will use discretion in the number of times their dog is used in the course of each year.

5 Members will not allow their bitches to whelp more than once in every twelve months or before two years of age or after the age of seven. A bitch will not have more than three litters during her lifetime.

6 Members will abide by the conditions for entry on to the puppy list.

7 Members shall ensure that any stock from which they breed shall be registered with The Kennel Club.

8 Members when advertising will not misrepresent themselves or their stock and will deal only in a fair and honest manner with clients who shall be advised of any fault the dog may have.

Clients buying stock shall be encouraged to present the dog to a veterinary surgeon within three days of purchase. Should a veterinary surgeon, at such an examination, advise that the dog is not suitable for the purpose for which it was bought, members will verify this option and, if necessary, take back such a dog and refund the purchase price.

9 Members will be encouraged to take advantage of any relevant, official scheme devised to test a dog's soundness.

10 Members will, when engaged in competitive events with their dogs, conduct themselves in such a way as not to bring discredit to the breed or Club and will demonstrate good sportsmanship at all times.

11 Repeated violations of this Code of Conduct may result in expulsion.

7 Showing

Choosing a Puppy to Show

Showing is great fun, but it has to be pointed out that it is a very expensive business these days and very time-consuming. All breeders get a thrill seeing a puppy that they have bred win at shows. It is often as rewarding as winning with your own dog, but you have to encourage people to show for their own benefit, not yours.

More experienced breeders will also give help and encouragement but are aware that not everyone wants to show just because they do. Therefore, do not push the new owner, but take pleasure from seeing your well-bred puppies going to a lovely home, where the family has researched the breed beforehand and are aware that the new puppy is capable of showing if required.

Rearing, the condition of the dog and presentation all play a great part in producing a champion. Having a 'perfect' puppy is not enough. Having said that, a breeder might be able to identify a puppy that appears more promising for show purposes than another at eight weeks.

A good breeder will not try to sell you an imperfect puppy; he will explain if a puppy is not up to show standard and why, but none of his puppies should be so unpresentable that you wouldn't want to take him home anyway.

There are several points which are relevant when seriously considering showing a Weimaraner. The breeder will stand the puppy in the show position for you, explaining the good and bad points of the puppy for showing. Obviously the puppy needs to be soundly made and typical of his breed.

You would not be able to show a Weimaraner with white on his toes successfully, except if he had a 'spur' on his heels. Although white hairs on the spurs do not meet the Standard, lots of very good dogs have them, so they are often accepted. Many people are needlessly worried by the sudden appearance of white hairs on puppies' tails. For some mysterious reason, all Weimaraner puppies develop white hairs on their tails at about four months of age. I was convinced that it was a reaction to the docking process. However, an undocked Weimaraner developed the same white hairs, disproving that theory. Don't be concerned, you will be able to show your puppy because this white hair on the tail will disappear within a few months.

He will need to have a correct bite. However, this cannot be guaranteed, as his bite may alter as his adult teeth emerge. If possible, check the dam and sire for their bite.

Weimaraners have fine, short coats with no protective undercoat, therefore cuts and tears in the coat resulting in scar tissue are not unheard of. A judge should not penalise a dog for a blemish or scar when judging him, unless it altered the dog's performance or detracted greatly from his beauty.

The puppy should look fit and healthy and he should have a certain amount of balance. He will go through various stages of being totally unbalanced, but if he is unbalanced at six to eight weeks, he will generally regain his balance later.

Training the Weimaraner for Showing

The Show Position

When you take him home, it is a good idea to teach him how to stand in the required show position. Weimaraners learn easily and quickly. Don't be heavy-handed when teaching him anything, but repeat the process often, otherwise he will quickly hate the procedure of learning to stand.

Stand a puppy for a short period once a day for the first week, decreasing the time spent as the weeks go on and he learns to do it. At four to five months stand him once a week for a longer period, say a couple of minutes. If you then take him on to match meetings do not stand him at home at all from five months onwards, otherwise he will find this repetitive, constant treatment boring instead of enjoyable.

To stand him properly, grasp the loose skin under his throat, talk gently to him and lift him between his back legs, so that he stands squarely. His head should be held high but level. His nose should not be stuck up in the air. Initially he will try to pull away defiantly. If you grit your teeth, pull and push at him and generally become flustered, he will get very excited and worried, then panic. If you become cross and disillusioned with him, he will be distressed and unhappy, and nothing will be achieved. If this happens, stop and do something else. Start again when you are in a more relaxed state of mind.

Hold him still, talking quietly and calmly to him all the time. If he pulls away, stay calm and put him back in position, telling him to stand. Keep the procedure very relaxed and determined. Your attitude must be I WILL WIN.

Always have the last word in everything when teaching your Weimaraner.

If you stand him and he moves before you want him to, don't excuse the situation by thinking you were going to release him anyway. He won't know what you are thinking; all he will understand is that if he struggles long enough he will get his own way and not have to do as you ask. Therefore, every time he has had enough he will move and refuse to do any more, struggling until you give in to him again, as you did the last time.

The puppy is happy to obey the handler's command, despite other distractions, because he has been carefully trained.

Don't say the same words every time you release him, because if you say those words he will move and you may not always require him to.

Stroke him gently so that when he is released from the standing position he doesn't jump up in excitement. Remember that when you are in the ring you will have to move him up and down the ring after standing him for the judge and it is not a good idea for him to go wild at that point. Never let him associate standing with a certain time or place or you will have difficulty getting him to do it at other times on request. He must learn to stand on request, whenever and wherever that may be – in fields, in the garden, on the pavement, etc. This discipline will make him more obedient and compliant and will be of mutual benefit.

The stubbornness of a Weimaraner responds well to black and white issues. There is no grey ground with him. If he sometimes does as you request and sometimes gets away with not doing it, he will very quickly

How and how not to stand your dog: (a) The bitch is over-stretched. (b) She is bunched up. (c) The back legs are too far back and she is leaning forward for biscuit. (d) The bitch has relaxed too much. (e) The bitch is too much on a slope, giving the incorrect topline. (f) The correct position, showing the bitch's beautiful outline and correct construction.

learn not to respect you and become defiant. Make him live by your rules, not you by his.

Once he knows how to stand and will do so easily only stand him at shows or match meetings. He will not give off his best otherwise. I often see bored puppies standing in the ring like little statues, totally unhappy with the proceedings. That is not the point of the exercise.

Young six- and seven-month-old puppies stand and show really well. After they become familiar with the process and gain confidence their behaviour can change: they might lean back and fidget or be naughty. They begin to show off with all the new dogs they meet and can become a nuisance.

When your youngster reaches this rebellious stage, you may think it best to fight with the dog. Really the best way to deal with the problem is to go back to stage one and try to make it fun again. Stand him when you are together enjoying yourselves; give him a treat for doing it properly and praise him. Don't do it too often and don't make a big drama out of it.

If he is pulling back and away from you, turn him round and stand him the opposite way. If he freezes as soon as you hold his head to stand him, take hold of his head as if to stand him, stroke him and talk to him, but don't stand him. He will relax and will not think you are trying to force him again. Make sure you are relaxed with him; if you are not, he will sense it and react accordingly.

If he leans back, catch up the lead tightly under his neck without strangling him, holding his head up. Stand his legs individually, talking

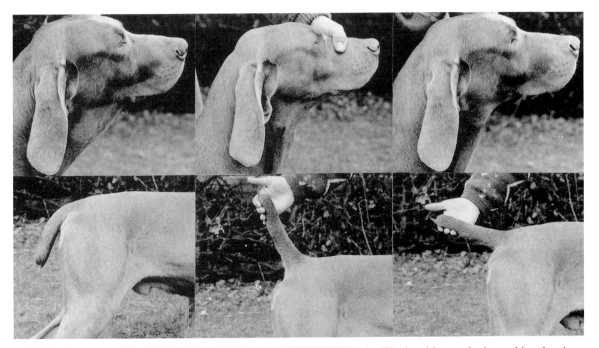

(a) The hand leaves the loose skin, showing that the dog is throaty. (b) The thumb over the nose alters the finished picture and obviously worries the dog, making him tense. (c) The hand is in the right place to show the correct head position. The nose is level, not up in the air or pointing down disinterestedly. (d) The tail is down. (e) The tail is held at too high an angle, which denotes aggression in a Weimaraner and is not wanted. (f) The tail is slightly up. The correct pose for the tail, it denotes confidence rather than aggression or shyness.

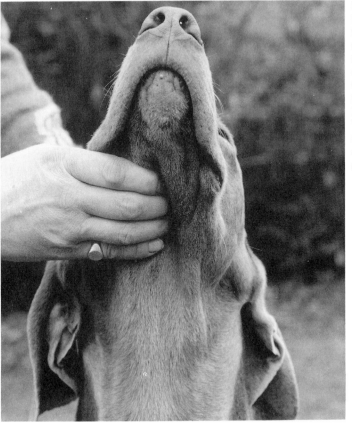

The correct position of the fingers, which will display the head properly.

(a) The wrong position of the head, this spoils the topline of the dog, as does the lead in the wrong place. (b) The correct head position with a clean line throughout. (c) This dog has poor front legs, weak pasterns and splayed feet. (d) Correct frontlegs, tight arched feet. (e) A cow-hocked Weimaraner. Note the lack of muscles in the thigh. (f) Strong hindquarters with good muscle. The hocks turn neither in nor out.

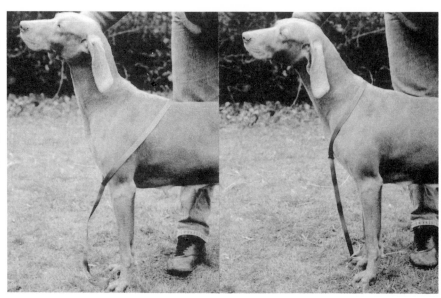

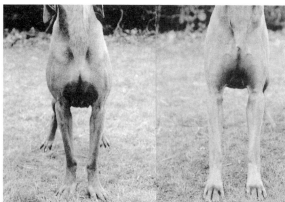

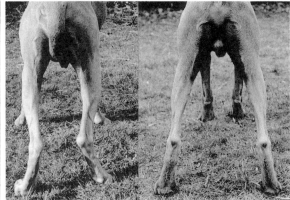

calmly to him all the time. When he is standing properly, scratch his tummy reassuringly.

If you are still having problems, another solution may be to change your stance. If you stand behind your dog he may stiffen. If you kneel behind him, he is less likely to realise what the situation entails and will relax. Changing the lead you use can also alter his reaction.

Reacting calmly and strongly to the situation will make him revert to his best behaviour all the more quickly. Do not build up a bad atmosphere, but change his habits gently.

Weimaraners never forget what they are taught as youngsters, they just go through annoying stages. If they know how to stand, but are asked too often, they become stale and rebel.

Moving in the Ring

The puppy needs to be taught to trot sensibly on the lead for showing. Treat this as a separate exercise from normal lead training and he will learn that this is another part of his job.

One problem when moving the dog for the judge, especially outside where wonderful smells prevail, is that the dog may want to put his nose to the ground and the poor handler trots down the ring struggling to keep the dog's head up. Obviously the judge cannot assess movement properly.

Think before you set off. If the dog has his head up initially, his desire to smell will be less. If you need to attract his attention to avert his thoughts from the ground, before you set off make sure that the lead is well up under his chin, not halfway down his neck.

Get his attention with a tit-bit, then pop it in your pocket so he doesn't jump about for it. Give a firm command and set off purposefully. When he gets going into his stride, you can loosen the lead so he can stride on.

It is often said that you cannot teach obedience training as well as show training to a dog. I think you can, as long as they are kept separate issues. This way the dog can identify the various training regimes. Never forget that showing is a hobby, for fun, so enjoy it.

Matches

I have mentioned match meetings or matches. They are usually held one evening a month in the local church or village hall. They are informal sessions run by the local dog club, where people can go to train and socialise their puppy. It is a useful procedure for novices, both human and canine.

Everyone is friendly and helpful and tries to put you at your ease. It doesn't matter if you make mistakes, everybody does. No one will laugh or frown on you; they might at themselves though. Treat it as it is meant, a pleasant social evening for you and your dog to enjoy. A good by-product of attending such evenings is that you are able to teach your dog good canine manners, including the proper behaviour when mixing with all and sundry.

Be aware of possible problems that can develop from bringing different breeds together in one place. For example, an English Setter is friendly and outgoing and, when he decides to play, may jump on top of the nearest dog. His is a breed that does not have a mean bone or thought and he expects every other dog to be the same.

A Weimaraner, on the other hand, is alert and aware and could react badly to the Setter jumping on him unprovoked. He was bred as a working hunting dog and he is used to bringing down large game. The Setter pouncing on him could very easily be interpreted by him as a threat. He might well round on the Setter and growl or even snap at him, responding to an instinct long bred into him.

Try to think one step ahead of him and prevent the situation from happening. If it does happen, don't get cross with the dog and his owner – no harm was meant – just monitor your dog and reassure him. He will quickly learn that other dogs are not aggressors and should be treated as friends. Never allow him to be snapped at in such a situation – he may be startled and his feelings hurt. He might think that the dog attacked him first for no good reason, so the next time he will be on his guard and get in first.

Weimaraners are a lovely breed, so understand their attributes and weaknesses and always try to promote them in a good light. Remember that they don't suffer fools or silly situations gladly. They shouldn't start a fight *ever*, but if they have to finish one they will. As owners we are their ambassadors and should act as such.

If you build a good, sound relationship with your dog, you will eventually be able to read each other's minds. You will sense each other's moods and be able to work together really well. When that happens nothing will give you such a feeling of satisfaction.

Types of Shows

The next step is to enter your puppy in a show. Six months is the earliest one can enter a dog for a show. All shows are registered with The Kennel Club. The different types of shows are as follows:

Match Meeting

This simply requires a licence. Two dogs are matched against each other and the ultimate winner is promoted as Best in Match.

Exemption Show

This is so called because it is exempt from Kennel Club rules in that a dog entered in it does not have to be registered with The Kennel Club. It usually has classes for pedigree dogs and novelty classes for dogs the judge would most like to take home with him or best-looking farm dog, etc.

These shows are fun events and prove to be useful training grounds for up-and-coming show dogs. They are often held in conjunction with a charity event or Young Farmers' Show in the summer months.

Sanction Show

This type of show is rapidly dying out, which is unfortunate because it provides a training ground for new judges and is the first really competitive show you can enter without feeling out of your depth. Dogs have to be entered before the event and have to be registered with The Kennel Club.

These shows are inexpensive to enter, but you have to be a registered member of the organising club or society. This is not expensive and gives a friendly atmosphere.

Only dogs up to post-graduate class are eligible to be shown at a Sanction Show. This means that a dog that has won five or more Firsts in post-graduate or higher classes cannot enter a Sanction Show and therefore the competition is not too fierce.

Limited Show

This is one step up from a Sanction Show. Entry is limited to dogs that have not won Challenge Certificates. Because Limited and Sanction Shows are smaller and less daunting than Open and Championship Shows, you have more opportunity to meet and talk with people who show other breeds. This can result in you learning some very useful pointers for both showing and judging.

Open Show

This is open to all, but dogs must be registered with The Kennel Club. Show Champions and Champions may enter, the only restriction is by definition of class: e.g. juniors must be under eighteen months of age, and post-graduates must not have won five or more First Prizes in post-graduate classes or higher.

More breed classes are available at Open Shows and this is beneficial to the Weimaraner. As the dog is relatively new to the British Isles, judges and show societies tended to fight shy of this unusual, contestable breed they know nothing about, and have never given the opportunities to Weimaraners that are available to Labradors, say, either in classes or wins. However, because the standard of handling and quality of the dogs is improving all the time, this attitude is changing rapidly.

It is very frustrating as an exhibitor always to have to show in a variety class. This is a class open to any breed of dog. It does not give the novice any idea how good his dog is or how he will stand up to competition against dogs in his own breed.

The judge of such a class should judge each dog against his Standard, not against the other breeds entered. The dog complying most closely to his Standard should win the class. Human nature being what it is means that most judges, especially those with only Open Show experience, will look more favourably on a breed that they are familiar with. A less popular breed will tend to be overlooked, because the judge would not want to put a bad specimen up and make himself look foolish.

The larger Open Shows used to be benched, but this is now dying out.

Mainly, I fear, because of the prohibitive cost. When a show is 'benched' it means that the dog is allocated a bench, which is like a partitioned kennel. The dog is fastened by a collar and chain to a clip on the bench and can rest there when not being exercised or shown.

Championship Show

This is the largest type of show, offering the most comprehensive range of breed classes. Only at this type of show are Challenge Certificates awarded.

The public instantly recognises Crufts Championship Show, which receives media attention. Named after Charles Cruft, a dog fancier who promoted dog shows, it was later taken over by The Kennel Club. Until 1991, Crufts had been held in February in London, but for various reasons it has moved to the National Exhibition Centre at Birmingham. (*Crufts: The Official History* is published by Pelham Books.)

Crufts has introduced a qualifying system, due to its massive number of entries. It is the show most people wish to win and aim for as their ultimate goal. You can only qualify to enter Crufts at a Championship Show, by winning in certain classes or by qualifying for entry in the Stud Book. The classes you must win are:

First, Second or Third in Minor Puppy
First, Second or Third in Puppy
First, Second or Third in Junior
First, Second or Third in Post-Graduate.

To qualify for Stud Book entry you must win:

First, Second or Third in a Limit Class
First, Second or Third in an Open Class
A Reserve Challenge Certificate
A Challenge Certificate.

These wins must be at a Championship Show. Once you have qualified for a place in the Stud Book, you are allocated a Stud Book number. This effectively qualifies that dog for Crufts and he need not qualify again as he will retain his Stud Book number until he dies. You may also qualify for a place in the Stud Book by winning the appropriate Field or Working Trials.

Crufts is not necessarily the biggest Championship Show, but it is the best known. It is always overcrowded with visitors from home and abroad. It involves a long and tiring day for both dog and handler. It is dirty and noisy, but despite all these disadvantages it has that certain something which no other show possesses.

Entering a Show

Lists of classes and the appropriate definitions are given in every show schedule. Read these carefully and enter accordingly, sticking to age classes where applicable or to just one class, so you don't get bored in a lot of classes under the same judge.

Age classes are listed up to special yearling usually. A special yearling is a dog not exceeding twenty-four calendar months of age on the first day of the show. Puppies grow, alter and mature at such a rate that it is unfair to lump them together in their formative year. Classes are not categorised by age when dogs are over two years old because by then the growth rate has stopped and they must compete on equal terms with dogs of different ages.

No puppy can be entered in or taken to a show when he is under six months of age. This is understandable, as he needs rest, sleep and creative play when he is young. Usually between four and six months he is so unbalanced by his growing body that it would not be fair to judge him in a show ring. At about four months of age his milk teeth fall out and are replaced by his adult teeth. When this occurs it is interesting to note that his feet seem to flatten and become ugly.

At six to nine months it is best to enter a Weimaraner in the Minor Puppy Class at Championship Shows, or Puppy Class at Open Shows. Don't over-show your puppy; he is a baby and will rapidly lose interest if you are not careful. Make it fun and light-hearted or you may end up with a reluctant exhibit in adult life.

Be sure that when entering a show you read the entry form carefully and in full. Make a note on the schedule of which classes you have entered. Keep the schedule safe so you don't lose it.

The best way to obtain a schedule is by purchasing a paper such as *Dog World* or *Our Dogs*. Both are weekly papers and can be ordered through or purchased at your newsagent's. If you are serious about showing your dog, then I suggest that you order the paper every week. Shows are advertised weekly and you can send a self-addressed envelope to the secretary for a schedule or telephone. Once you are on the society mailing list you will be sent a schedule automatically.

Awards

Challenge Certificate

This is a large green-edged card that is awarded only at Championship Shows and is given to the best of each sex. It is also referred to as the C.C. or 'Ticket'. Three C.C.s awarded to one dog by three different judges, subject to Kennel Club approval, qualify that dog as a Champion. Gundogs become Show Champions (Sh.Ch.). A gundog becomes a Champion when or if he gains a Show Gundog certificate or an award at least to a Certificate of Merit at a Kennel Club-recognised Field Trial.

Field Trial Champion

Otherwise known as FTCh., this is awarded to a Weimaraner if he wins a Championship Trial run for Hunt, Point, Retrieve (HPR) breeds, or to a dog that received First at two different Field Trials in an Open Stake in which there are no fewer than ten runners. An Open Stake is open to all and is not restricted by age or wins.

At the time of writing, Weimaraners have only one such FTCh., a wonderful achievement by both dog and handler/owner. He is FTCh. Wobrooke of Fleetapple, owned and handled by Mrs D. Arrowsmith. A Dual Champion is a dog which has become a Field Trial Champion and a Show Champion – an achievement never attained by a Weimaraner in this country as yet.

Junior Warrant

This is awarded to a dog gaining twenty-five points or more between the ages of twelve and eighteen months. Three points are awarded for each First Prize in a Breed Class at a Championship Show, where C.C.s are awarded for the breed. One point is awarded for each First Prize in a Breed Class at an Open Show.

This particular rule only came into effect in January 1990. Prior to that time Junior Warrants were awarded in the same way, but varied in the age allowance – between the ages of six and eighteen months.

It is not fair to push a young dog beyond his limit. Hopefully, the new rule will prevent this happening in future and let the youngster enjoy his first taste of the ring.

Arriving at the Show

The best way to become familiar with showing is to visit a local show, watch and listen. Get the feel of the shows, then you can go home and enter the classes you feel best suited for.

You will be apprehensive at your first show. Ask other Weimaraner owners for their help; on the whole they will be only too pleased to offer whatever assistance they can. Just remember not to pester them when they are obviously busy or about to go into the ring.

It isn't the way you stand or dress that makes you a good handler, but your ability to attain an affinity with the dog you are handling and to respond to him. Dogs, especially Weimaraners, know what you are thinking and feeling – it travels through the lead to them – so try to keep calm when showing. The easiest way of achieving this is to organise yourself so that the opportunity for things to go wrong and fluster you is less likely.

Plan your route to the show well beforehand. Fill the car with petrol and pack your show bag, making sure you have the following items:

> Ring clip for your number
> Pen, to mark the winners in your catalogue
> Exhibitors' passes
> Chamois leather, to wipe the dog
> Tit-bits and treats for the dog
> Benching chain and collar
> Rug for use on the bench
> Towel for rubbing him down if it is wet or muddy. If it is hot you can cool him down with water, then dry him, or even soak the towel to cool him.
> Food for the dog
> Poop scoop for excrement and a number of plastic bags
> If you have time or space, anything you might need for yourself.

Make sure you arrive at the show with lots of time to spare. This will allow you time to steady yourself, have something to eat and prepare yourself for the day ahead.

Exercise your dog and clear up any excrement with your poop scoop. Venues are hard enough for the organisers to find without having the anti-dog brigade baying because of unhygienic and health-hazardous waste being left by entrants.

Benching

All Championship Shows are benched and dogs should be benched at all times, except when they are in the ring or being exercised. Make sure you familiarise your dog with the process of being benched when he is a youngster. At the first few shows he attends he will be far happier with you than on his own. Take him round the show and acclimatise him to the sights and sounds and to all the bustle and excitement.

When he has been in the ring and the day is drawing on, take him to the bench and secure him. Stay with him; some dogs settle far more easily than others. When he lies down and goes to sleep, move out of his sight, but stay in the vicinity in case he wakes. He may be frightened and try to pull the bench down or throw himself off it and hurt himself. He may just make as much noise as possible, and you and he will not be very popular. Every time he is benched, leave him for a slightly longer period. After four or five sessions on the bench he will be fine.

Fasten him to the bench on a short chain, so he doesn't get off the bench or lunge out. Even when he is used to being left, you must check him regularly, to make sure that he is all right and does not bother anyone. I generally check from a distance so that he can't see me and I don't disturb him needlessly. Remember to exercise him regularly: it is very difficult to plait your legs on a bench.

Weimaraners are a very protective breed and they can be sharp or aggressive when benched. This proves to be a very difficult trait to break, as they don't usually behave in such a manner when you are with them.

If your dog behaves this way, wait round a corner for him to start behaving badly, then get to him speedily and smack him with your hand, telling him a firm 'NO'. Retreat swiftly and wait for him to start again. The other alternative is to ask neighbouring owners to watch and shout to you if he starts misbehaving or to keep their dogs a little further away so he has no need to fight for his territory.

Try not to be irritated if people are cross with you when your dog behaves in such a way. The victim could be shocked and, after all, it is your dog that is at fault. Apologise and tell them that you don't like this trait any more than they do, but you find it difficult to stop. They may even offer some sound advice on how to stop it. You should not be cross with other people's dogs for acting in the same fashion.

Do persevere when benching your dog, however difficult and trying it may be. Ultimately your dog will be far happier benched, where he can rest in peace after what may have been a long journey. If you try to trail him round with you all day, he will tire and become crotchety, which will do neither him nor you any good. He is then far more likely to snap at passing dogs – earning him, you and the breed a bad name.

In the Ring

Remove your dog from the bench with time to spare when he is to go into the ring. He may wish to relieve himself or stretch his legs if he is stiff from being still a long time. A brisk trot round will revive him and loosen him up.

It is often a good idea to take him to a quiet spot and stand him in the show position so he knows what is going on. Trot him up and down a couple of times to gauge what kind of mood he is in. If he is full of exuberance, you will know you have to settle him when you are in front of the judge. On the other hand, if he is having an off day and is lethargic, it gives you a chance to wind him up and jolly him along.

Watch the class before yours, it will give you an idea of what is expected from you by that particular judge: some move you more than others; some expect you to move first. If you have an idea of the format beforehand, you won't be caught off-guard.

Look at the ring and find the best spot for you. If your dog is up to size, you may want to stand in a dip, because if you stand on a hill he will look bigger. If the hall has dark spots make sure you are in plenty of light so that you can be seen.

Check that you know your number, so that when you enter the ring you will be able to recite it immediately to the steward and not waste his time. Stand your dog, so that when the judge surveys the ring you are not dithering about. Remember first impressions count for a lot.

As the person in front of you is finishing his turn in front of the judge, stand your dog ready to be viewed. When the judge requests you to do something, obey him quickly, quietly and efficiently.

If he asks you to show your dog the opposite way round, do it, even if it means standing with your back to the judge while placing your dog and then changing sides to face him. It is not your place to question why a judge requests you to do anything. It is against Kennel Club rules to hold a conversation with the judge, unless he specifically asks you something or you need to point something out to him.

The choice was yours to enter a class under that judge, not his. Don't complain if you don't like him or what he does. You pay your money and you take your choice.

Some judges expect you to be a competent handler; they might not be as good a handler as they expect you to be, but they are not the ones exhibiting. Your dog must not interfere with any of the other dogs in the ring. The other dogs might take offence and trouble might start. A handler might just have set his dog up and your animal sniffing his rear might spook him.

Keep an eye on the judge at all times when in the ring. Don't waste your time and money by chatting idly and letting your dog lounge. You will be in the ring for approximately half an hour – use the time well. You might be in a class of twenty dogs, ten of which are good. The judge might take to splitting hairs to reach a decision or one dog might stand out for style and quality. Every time the judge sees the dog, he should be looking his best and this will be to his advantage, but don't keep him standing tense or he will become bored.

A dog often moves just when the judge is looking at him. Many times handlers come out of the ring complaining that their dog has done just that. They then think that they would have won if he had not moved at that moment. The majority of judges are not so hard or inexperienced that they would reduce the placing of a dog just because he moved at the vital moment. They will already have weighed up the merits of each dog and one wrong move should not prove disastrous.

The dog moves in response to you. When the judge moves towards you, you become nervous and start thinking, 'Gosh, I hope he doesn't move'. The dog senses your apprehension, becomes restless and moves.

Another time when things go wrong for no apparent reason is when you have won. It is usually the male Weimaraner that begins to bark and jump about. He is happy that you are pleased with him for winning and gets over-excited and shows his pleasure by jumping about. Another dog may go on the defensive and then you have the makings of a potential disaster.

Always be polite to the judge and the other handlers in the ring. If you lose, make a point of congratulating the winner. You may feel that your dog is superior, but the decision is the judge's. The perfect dog has not been born. Each and every one has attributes and faults, some just have more attributes than others, which is why they win more consistently.

Breeders who consistently breed good stock have spent years developing their line and type. Speaking to such people you can learn such a lot. They are usually very down to earth and don't boast about how successful their dogs are, nor do they need to have pictures in every dog publication every time their dogs win. It is not necessary because their record speaks for itself.

Don't be in a hurry to win all the prizes as soon as you start showing or be disappointed if you don't. All dogs differ; some mature early, become balanced earlier and therefore win. Others are leggy or short of body when young but blossom into super dogs later on. Weimaraners as a breed tend to mature later rather than earlier.

Presentation

Presentation is important for the dog and you. The dog should be in good condition and of good stature. If he is a bit short of muscle get him out and give him some work. A good mix of free running and road work will tone him up and help keep his feet tight. The feet can become flat if the dog lacks exercise or is exercised only on soft ground.

Weimaraners do not need to be bathed often as they are by nature clean animals. Mud can be brushed off easily with a body brush as it dries. If they are in good health and condition it shows in their coat and general appearance. We only bath our dogs if they have been in foul water or if the weather has been dry over a long period and they need freshening up. If they are bathed too often, you could risk losing all the natural oil from their coats and, having no undercoat, they really need it.

Cut your dog's nails, check his teeth and ears are clean, but don't poke about, and he should be ready for the off.

It is important that you are presentable; think about what you would like to wear, then think again to see if it is really suitable. Remember that you will be wearing the clothes you choose most of the day. If you are travelling in them as well, you will have to wear them for an even longer period. Make sure you are comfortable and relaxed in them, or you will not be able to concentrate properly on the job you have to do. Try to be clean and well groomed. Do your dog justice by being tidy.

Remember that what looks nice when you are stationary might flap in the dog's face when on the move, or cover him when you bend down. Whistles might look effective in the ring, but clatter about when you are running with your dog, causing distractions. Save them for the Field Trial. Some colours might complement the dog, others will really clash. Don't wear something outrageous, it will only take people's eyes off the dog.

Shoes are another consideration. I hate to see ladies wearing stilettos with a dog on a lead. They could easily be knocked off balance and tread on his foot, leading to untold pain and possibly even broken bones in the dog's foot. Flat walking shoes are ideal, as are trainers. If you do stand on his feet, the damage won't be so severe.

The wax jacket proves invaluable at summer shows that are held outside, with tents providing the wet weather arrangements. Of course, you still have to get to the wet weather ring from the benching tent.

I prefer showing in the rain outside to bringing my dog into a dark and badly lit tent. Although the Weimaraner has a short coat which represents no problem in bad weather, in dark surroundings the dog disappears. The rings tend to be small and, as the Weimaraner is a big dog, they don't give you the opportunity to move him properly.

A dog show is, in reality, a canine beauty contest. The dog is presented as a correctly constructed member of his type of breed, able to work in the job he was bred for. Showing is useful for the breed in that it maintains the Breed Standard.

I have watched certain breeds in the Gundog Group being split into show or work dogs and the difference between the two is quite alarming. We do not have that problem in our breed because so many people work as well as show their dogs.

If you show seriously, it can be unfair to keep dogs who will not be shown and therefore not stimulated fully. They will be mentally neglected because you will be so busy with the others. Weimaraners need a lot of mental as well as physical stimulation and you must give them this attention even if they are not going to the show with you.

Judging

The natural progression from showing is judging. As with showing, it is best to start your judging experience with match meetings.

Your main duty is to go over the dog and give him confidence in the procedure so that when he attends a show, he will accept his job and let the judge assess him properly. Relax and enjoy the proceedings and use the experience to your benefit and to gain confidence in yourself.

It is amazing how you can sometimes end up giving the Best In Match award to a breed you know nothing about. You might think it a fluke to choose a good dog from a different breed. It is far more likely that you have started to develop an eye for a 'good' dog, despite not knowing the idiosyncrasies of that breed.

It is useful to attend seminars on different breeds if you have an interest in dogs and judging. Seminars usually have four to six people who are knowledgeable about a breed or a certain aspect of dogdom. Each speaker will cover a different aspect of that breed. One may speak of what is looked for in that dog in the show ring. There might be an all-rounder to give his views. Another might discuss the working side of the breed and points as to whether the breed is veering more to the show and away from its working origins, or whether the breed is splitting into two types of the same breed, working and showing. Some seminars offer the experience of going over a live specimen. This would be invaluable to a novice judge. It would be well worthwhile attending, so watch for advertisements in the dog papers.

You have to learn how and why you take hold of the dog when judging. You hold the head so that you can manipulate it to see the expression properly. You will be able to measure the length of the ear with the other hand.

Then you examine the mouth for the bite. On a hot day you may wish to take hold of the flew, to see if it is too short or snipey, or if the dog is just pulling his lip back while panting in the heat.

One hand holds the head, while the other runs down the neck, gauging its strength, then to the point of the withers to make sure the shoulders are the correct distance apart. They should not be touching or overly wide. The hands can be taken down either side of the rib cage to see if the ribs are well sprung or fat.

You will be able to feel if the body reaches down to the point of the elbow. In a short-coated breed this can be seen, whereas in a long-haired variety it generally has to be felt.

Feeling over the loins proves if there is strength there. Your hand tells you where the end of the rib is, showing the length of the loin. If the dog is tense and standing straight in the stifle, running your hand down the stifle joint will indicate if there is a good bend. The buttocks will show the quality of the muscling when touched. If the dog is not in condition, your hands will feel it. The best way to assess if the dog is true and entire is to feel.

Some judges hardly lay a finger on the dogs. It is not fair to judge in this fashion. Remember that exhibitors pay to have you give your opinion of their dog and it is therefore only good manners to give that dog your very best attention. You might have dismissed him in your head, but you have to give him his due.

It is useful to work out a pattern to work by that you feel comfortable with when judging. When you have found a pattern that you are happy with, stick to it and it will become second nature to you. Nothing instills doubt in the exhibitor more than a judge who changes his technique halfway through his class of dogs.

The dogs will be stacked for you to assess as a group at the beginning of the class. Walk down the line, briefly looking at heads, bodies and hindquarters. In a puppy class, if the ring is of adequate size, send the dogs round. This serves to settle the nerves of both dog and handler. Then go over each dog in turn, move the dog in a triangle, then straight up the ring and back down. This helps show the movements from all angles; you don't need to move the dog constantly.

You may wish to move a dog just before you make your final choice, just to refresh your memory. By the time you reach the stage of placing the dogs, you should know which ones appeal to you and why. The final assessment does not need to take ages. The more you look at this stage, the more faults you see and the harder and more confusing the job becomes.

Be decisive, it is your day; do the job as best you can. Don't judge a dog by his faults, all dogs have faults. It is far better to place a dog on his merits.

Critiques on placings at shows are printed in the dog press weekly. People love to read about their dogs and why they have won or been placed, so write a critique on the dogs of a class you have judged. At Open Shows only the first placement is written about; at Championship Shows, the first two are.

You must write the dog's number in your judging book. This is given to you by the secretary on the day of the judging. It is useful to put why you like your winners in the book, in brief. Then, at a later stage, you will be able to check a dog against your notes and number.

Very often new judges are not told to keep all judging books and catalogues. You will need them at a later date for checking dates and entries for The Kennel Club. They have a questionnaire for judging at Championship Shows, and keeping a judging book of appointments means you can check easily to see if you have judged the required amount of classes needed. The Kennel Club can and does ask for proof of the shows you have judged. The books and catalogues give that proof.

Your judging diary also helps when a club invites you to judge, as you will have to write back. If you accept, you are effectively making a contract with them. You will not be able to change your mind at a later date or you will be in serious trouble with The Kennel Club for breach of contract. If you are ill and another judge has to be appointed, The Kennel Club must be informed. Your reasons will be noted and taken into consideration.

The society may ask you to refrain from judging at another show in their area for a limited time. Obviously to judge several shows in the same radius at the same time would deplete the entrants for each show. This applies to Open and smaller shows.

You are not allowed by Kennel Club rules to accept appointments to judge the same breed at a Championship Show where C.C.s are on offer within nine months.

8 Shooting Over Your Weimaraner

The splitting of some gundog breeds into two 'types' – working and showing – urges me to try to preserve the Weimaraner as a dual-purpose breed. It is always a loss if a breed of dog loses its instincts and can no longer fulfil its purpose in life. I feel very strongly that lovers of Weimaraners should work together for the good of the breed and should not condemn those who specialise in a particular area, be it working, showing, field trialing or just enjoying the animal as a pet.

The shooting season starts at the end of the summer and only lasts a short while, whereas the show season is at its height during the summer. This means that both can be enjoyed with a modicum of success, as has been proved on a number of occasions.

This chapter has been written by a novice in field trialing to help those who are thinking about embarking on shooting over their Weimaraner. There are many excellent books detailing the idiosyncrasies of field trialing and how to train your dog to a very high standard. I have found *The All-Purpose Gundog*, written by David Layton, to be the most useful and the easiest to interpret. It is specifically written for and about the German Short-Haired Pointer (GSP) but it is very applicable to the Weimaraner.

If you wish to field trial your Weimaraner it is best to find a gundog training class. This will help you to start out on the right footing and stay on it. If you learn bad habits, they are difficult, if not impossible, to eradicate at a later stage.

Training class information is readily available through The Weimaraner Club of Great Britain and The Weimaraner Association. Both of these clubs actively encourage the working of this breed in the manner for which they were bred.

You might not wish to compete with your dog, but classes may be invaluable for you both if you wish only to go beating with him or to rough shoot. For the serious field trialer, your work may be harder with a Weimaraner. He is not as natural in HPR competition work as, say, the GSP. However, the Weimaraner has many attributes, so don't feel despondent if you wish to work him.

Much can be achieved with Weimaraners, as has been proven by the many

FTCh. Wobrooke of Fleetapple, owned by Di Arrowsmith – the only Field Trial Champion Weimaraner.

who have competed and won awards. Take, for instance, Di Arrowsmith's FTCh. Wobrooke of Fleetapple.

On the Continent, dogs are graded against their own breed when judged. In this country, the Weimaraner is one of only six breeds of dog listed as HPRs for the purpose of field trialing. The six breeds which comprise this group are the Brittany Spaniel, German Short-haired Pointer, German Wire-haired Pointer, Hungarian Vizsla, Large Musterlander and the Weimaraner. All of these breeds are active, intelligent and capable of competing in the show ring and the field.

The main difference between the GSP and the Weimaraner when working is that the Weimaraner is slower at covering the ground. This is useful in thick cover, but can waste time on open ground. The Weimaraner also has a tendency to ground scent, which may be derived from his probable hound ancestry. Ground scenting is a disadvantage, as it means he will be almost on the bird before he scents it, and therefore there is a risk of it being disturbed. When air scenting, the dog takes the bird's scent from the air and is aware of it from a greater distance.

Whether rough shooting, or on a driven shoot, as a gun or beater, the thing you both need is to be fit and to have stamina. Don't expect your dog to enjoy a whole day on a grouse moor if he has only had half an hour's exercise the week before. It may sound simple, but people do seem to take a dog's fitness for granted. You and your dog will both benefit from regular exercise.

The Shooting Season

This is another fundamental fact which every experienced shooting man takes for granted, but one which you really need to know – the dates of the shooting season.

The Season	Open	Close
Grouse & Ptarmigan	12 August	10 December
Snipe	12 August	31 January
Partridge	1 September	1 February
Pheasant	1 October	1 February
Woodcock & Capercaillie	1 October	31 January
Woodcock in Scotland	1 September	31 January

No one ever shoots on a Sunday, Christmas Day or a Bank Holiday. If the 'Glorious 12th' for instance fell on a Sunday, the grouse shooting would start on the 13th.

Gamekeepers are employed to care for and control the game, to preserve and protect them all the year through. The open and closed seasons are there for the protection of the game, giving them time to breed and flourish. Much money is injected into the sport by shooting folk for this end.

Choosing the Puppy

Whatever aspect of field work you wish to participate in with your Weimaraner, your first step is to acquire your puppy. It is not absolutely necessary to go to a kennel specialising in working dogs if you want to shoot over a Weimaraner. However, you do need a well-established, experienced breeder with a sound reputation.

Discuss your future requirements with the breeder. As the puppies develop and mature over the weeks prior to leaving for their new home, the breeder will build up a knowledge of which puppy is showing an aptitude for working. One might show his aptitude as a thinking puppy with his nose to the ground, ferreting out different smells, but he might not be the biggest nor the liveliest.

Avoid a nervous or shy puppy. The puppy needs to be bold and self-assured. By seven to eight weeks of age, the puppy you have your eye on should be inquisitive, watchful and daring to go that bit further than the others in the litter. He will be the one picking things up and proudly carrying off his prize.

Training for Field Trialing

As soon as you take the puppy home, begin training him. He should have inherited all the instincts he will require. Your job is to bring these instincts to the fore and make them work for him. Initial training should be in the form of a game to teach him good habits for his future work so that it will be a pleasure for you both and he will be more willing to respond to you.

Working your dog is like showing him successfully. It cannot be done by taking him out only once a week or less. It requires hard work from you and the building up of a deep relationship and understanding between the two of you, which will create mutual respect.

As he develops he will learn the correct way of doing things if you bring him on properly. Don't make the learning games too long or he will become bored and start to hate them. You will lose the rapport you have built up with him and unintentionally you will be fighting against each other instead of working together. Learn to recognise the signs. Stop and start from the beginning, so that you both forget the bad experience and can work together again. This is important to learn in any aspect of dog ownership, especially when you are working closely together, as when shooting.

Before you take him out, your puppy requires vaccinating. The weeks preceding the completion of this process, when the puppy is confined, can be tedious for you both. However, there are various games you can both enjoy. They will start you off in the right way so that you can proceed with the more serious work later on. Chapter 4 explains various methods of training, some of which are applicable to the gundog. Teaching him his name and to sit are obviously very useful. Remember to proceed gently at this stage.

Lead Training

Do your lead training in whichever way suits you best. Remember, however, that you must never allow him to pull at the lead, ever. If he walks sensibly on the lead, it will be easier to obtain the same degree of control when he is off it.

The dog should be taught to walk on the left side of his handler and should not be allowed to sniff the ground. He should concentrate on walking. The left side is preferable, because when he is working the handler will be carrying his gun in his right hand, unless of course he is left-handed. It is far easier for all concerned if the dog always walks on the opposite side to the gun.

Once he has been trained to walk sensibly on a lead, it may be a good idea to use a rope lead on him. This is useful for a working dog for a variety of reasons. Being soft, it will not rub either your hand or the dog's skin when wet. It is light and you don't need the extra weight of a choker when walking miles over rough terrain. It is easily put on or taken off the dog should the need arise when he is working.

Always ensure that the lead is placed on the dog the correct way up. The metal ring through which the lead passes should be on the side of the handler, with the lead connected to the ring going under the dog's throat. The lead then comes over the dog's neck and is passed through the ring, so that when the lead is tightened it will release easily. If the lead is put on upside down the reverse happens and the lead will not release easily when required, which could choke the dog.

The 'Sit' Command

It is best to teach him to sit on command while he is on the lead. When you stop walking, say 'sit', lift the left hand, palm forward and stamp the ground with the left foot. If he doesn't sit when asked, gently but determinedly press down on his bottom and give the command to sit. This can be done at any time, anywhere. In fact the more varied the circumstances the better, so he will not think that he has to sit only in a training environment.

He will soon get used to seeing the hand raised and the foot stamped and will soon associate these actions with sitting. This proves invaluable at the later stage when you are out working with your dog. You won't want to frighten the game by shouting to your dog to sit. All you should need to do to be obeyed automatically is to raise your hand. If you aren't obeyed, then your training has not been successful and you need to start at the beginning again. The same applies if your dog is at your side and cannot see your hand – the vibration from the stamp of your foot should be enough to make him sit so you don't alert the game.

Don't make him sit too long in the initial stages of training or he may wish to lie down. I was always taught never to allow a dog to lie on the sit command, because when he is in thick cover he will not be able to see you and your commands therefore will not be adhered to.

It is necessary that your dog sit on command, wherever he is and under any circumstances – not just at your side. A good time to effect a response to your command is at meal times, when his interest is focused on food. If you ask him to sit he will, in eager anticipation of his meal coming more quickly if he obeys. If he already sits on command then, while holding his dish, hold your hand up palm outfacing and stamp your foot, saying 'sit'. This will condition him to associate both words and actions with the need to sit. If he doesn't want to sit, calmly hold the dish, say 'sit' and gently press his bottom down until he does.

The 'Stay' Command

After he knows the expected response to the 'sit' command, you can begin to incorporate 'stay' into the command. After the sit command is obeyed, continue to hold the dish as you say 'stay' firmly. When he responds correctly praise him.

As he progresses, put the dish down, holding you hand up and palm forward. Again restrict the time, as he is only a baby. However, you must have the last word or he will think he can move at his will, not yours. As he grasps the meaning of 'stay', you can practise in the field.

Leave his lead on, which will give him the feeling that you are still in control of him. Ask him to sit using your hand action, then with a good firm 'stay' back away from him, keeping your eyes on him at all times for any movement. Don't become over-confident, or train for too long on one exercise – short and frequent should be your motto. If he follows you, say 'NO', return him to the original sit position and repeat the process so that you have the last word.

As with any training, especially where a feeding bowl is used as an aid, make sure that there are no distractions or competition from another dog. It is not fair to ask him to concentrate on your commands when he feels that there is another dog hovering around, ready to pinch his tea at the first opportunity.

When teaching him to stay, don't be tempted to call him to you when he has completed his test correctly. This could encourage him to break his stay. Don't worry that he will not come when called at a later date. It is a natural instinct for him to come to you if he loves and respects you; he will want to be with you.

Once you have mastered 'stay' when backing away from him, you should then move towards him with the hand still raised. As you approach, calmly say 'stay' and walk closely past him. Eventually you should be able to make him sit and to walk in a large circle round him without him moving. It is rather like lungeing a horse. He will most likely watch your every movement. This is acceptable so long as he doesn't attempt to move. It means that he is alert and concentrating on the job at hand.

As he progresses, you will be able to lengthen the distance between you and the time of the exercise. If he moves at all, ALWAYS restart the exercise. Remember not to make the whole thing too long and boring for him. Always finish on a good note and make him feel he has achieved something for you and himself. That way he will remember the right way to do things and be eager to do them for you.

When you feel confident, start to issue commands without the lead. Do it right from the beginning, perfecting 'sit' without a lead, before moving on to the next stage.

Use of the Whistle

When working your dog, you will require a pea whistle and a shrill panic whistle. The latter is used rarely and only in a panic situation. For instance, if the dog takes flight after a hare and ignores your 'stop' command, the shrill sound of the panic whistle should be enough to jolt him into obedience.

A whistle is used when working because shouting frightens game unaccustomed to the sound of voices. A whistle blends in with the sounds of the countryside and the birds tend to ignore it. The whistle also has the advantage of being less stressful on the handler. Shouting up hill and down dale is not easy and as the whole point of the exercise is to enjoy the job and unwind, a whistle is a very user-friendly aid.

When asking your dog to sit, substitute 'sit' with a long blow on the whistle, but continue with the hand and foot movements. If he doesn't obey, blow again and press down on his bottom.

It is most impressive if a dog does as he is told by whistle command, especially when out walking or when there are other dogs about.

Recall

When sit and stay have been fully mastered, the next stage is recall. After he has sat and stayed, make sure you have his complete attention. He won't return to you if he feels there is something far more interesting going on elsewhere and will run off to investigate. This will only serve to instil bad habits in him that are very hard to break.

When you have his complete attention, call his name and tell him to 'come'. At the same time slap each thigh with outstretched hands and encourage him back to you. Once he has the hang of it, start to use the whistle. Sound two short blasts, accompanied by the actions, instead of using your voice.

When he is young and/or a novice, don't call him back if he is dashing off after a rabbit, because he will not come back. He must be conditioned to think that every time he hears a recall signal he must return without fail. Therefore, when he gets older and comes across a distraction, he will ignore it and answer your command as he always has done.

If, on the other hand, you call and he decides not to come to you, but runs off instead, never run after him, unless there is a danger of him running on to a road or injuring himself, and then only as a last resort. By running after him, you imply that it is a game and that you are chasing him as part of that game.

If you run or move in the other direction, this may unnerve him into thinking you don't want him. He will invariably lose confidence in the situation and come after you. When he reaches you, praise him for returning and only occasionally give him a treat, otherwise he will expect one every time. Once he understands what is expected of him when recalled, do the exercises sparingly. Concentrate on 'sit' and 'stay', as these are more alien to him.

Steadiness

The degree of obedience necessary for a gundog is not as great as for that of a Working Trial dog. I am told that an obedience trained dog will not always go on well enough in a Field Trial environment. The one thing he *must* do though is *stop*.

If you are working your dog and he doesn't respond to the stop whistle he will ruin the Field Trial for everyone else by dispersing the game. He will be very unpopular on a rough or driven shoot, because he will flush game out of range of the guns.

Training your dog to be steady and to stop is a progression from the earlier training to sit, and it takes time and patience. He should understand and totally comply with the sit whistle and then, keeping him steady, he should be whistled down from a distance, while he is concentrating on you.

Over a period of time, as he responds confidently to the sit whistle from a close distance, you should be able to stop him with your whistle from doing whatever he is doing. One situation in which this steadiness will prove useful is when your dog comes into contact with fur (i.e. rabbits and hares). A dog must not chase fur. He has to be taught to leave a rabbit or hare.

I have found that covering a dummy with a rabbit skin and attaching a strong piece of elastic to it proves a useful training aid. This should only be used when control is assured and the dog is old enough, so that he can cope mentally with what is expected of him.

In this exercise your dog should be fifty yards down the field, with a colleague with the dummy at the other end. The end of the elastic is secured to the ground and pulled at floor level across the path that the dog will take when asked to retrieve. Another handler hides in the side holding the fur-covered dummy, pulling the elastic taut. The dummy is thrown and the dog is asked to 'on and fetch'. As he sets off, the fur dummy is released, shooting across in front of him. He is asked to leave, go on and retrieve. I have found this exercise very useful in making the dog very steady on fur.

Hunting On and Quartering

It is very important if you wish to shoot over your dog that he has the ability to hunt on. 'Hunting on' means that the dog will use his nose and hunt, rather than sniff and potter about looking for his handler. I have learned from those experienced in and enthusiastic about Field Trials that it is the most important exercise required from a shooting dog. If you think about it, if your dog doesn't have the ability to hunt, then he cannot find game. You will have nothing to shoot, and therefore your day will have been wasted.

While walking over land with your puppy, don't call him back, but let him run on. Don't let him disappear completely, but if you have trained him properly, he will not leave you for any length of time.

When a dog hunts he takes scent of the game from the wind. In simple terms the idea is for him to hunt into the wind, moving across the beat – the area of ground to be hunted by the dog – from side to side scenting for game. This is called quartering. He should move across the beat between the guns, but not passing through the guns' line of fire.

The dog must not gallop off, but hunt the ground within range of the gun, otherwise he could put up game which is out of range. If he hunts on out of sight and goes on point, it is of no use to you. You have no idea where he is and therefore cannot respond to his point by flushing and shooting the game.

You may often see your pet quartering when out walking with him. You may not recognise it as such, but once you do you will notice his pattern of covering the ground. You can shape this instinct into a more uniform pattern by understanding the winds and helping him. For example, the wind coming straight at you when you stand still is known as a 'head wind'.

You have to think where the game is most likely to be. If the day is warm and sunny, the game will probably be basking in the sun. If it is cold and windy, the game will most likely be sheltering under hedges and the like. Your dog will need encouraging to move faster over the open ground so as not to waste time. He will need to check hedges and coppices thoroughly.

You must send your dog out, normally to the left. The ideal beat would be not more than twenty yards each side of the handler. As he goes backwards and forwards across the field you should encourage him with a clear hand signal at the end of the beat to show him the way. For instance, move off to the left, making a distinct action with your left arm out, palm upwards, so that it can be seen easily. A short pip on the whistle means listen, concentrate, turn and cover the other side of the beat. Be prepared to move to encourage him to go on across the beat, taking the wind and any scent as he goes.

Don't forget your job and run in front of him on the beat or you will

This puppy is having his pointing instincts brought out by a 'pheasant' dummy.

disturb what game there may be. In fact, during the initial training, it is best to use a field clean of game. It avoids distractions.

Once he knows the routine, your dog can be introduced to quartering on land with game. As his instincts develop, he will realise why he is being asked to do this job. He will then hunt on with a reason, but you will have the ability to control him, as you will have trained him well.

The dog is required to quarter with the intention of finding game. Once found, he must not flush the game until you are ready and in a position to shoot it. This is where his pointing instinct is needed.

Pointing

If a dog goes on point, he is telling you that there is game present. The dog goes rigid, like a stone statue, when on point. It looks as though you could pick the dog up and move him, without him moving a muscle; it is fascinating to watch, however many times you see it.

Pointing cannot be taught, but it can be encouraged. Cover a dummy with the wings of a pheasant and attach to it a fishing line of string tied to a long stick. The puppy is interested in the 'pheasant' dummy and dashes on to retrieve it. When he gets close, snatch the dummy away. The puppy stops and looks for the pheasant; keep repeating this until the puppy begins to realise that he must creep up on the pheasant or it will fly off.

As the dog creeps up stay close to him and say 'steady, steady'. Gently stroke all the way along his back, talking soothingly and making him steady.

When you are out on walks, if the puppy comes across game and stops, encourage him with the word 'steady'. If you are unlikely to come across game, you could plant it. Put some form of game in a cage and hide it in the grass so that it cannot be seen. Come back later with the dog and let him work into the wind, so that he will have the chance of scenting the game. This should have the desired effect of bringing him on point.

He must always be encouraged to remain steady and not run in and flush until you are ready for him to do so. When the puppy is older and he has been carefully introduced to the sound of gunfire, he should be taught to drop to that sound, so that when the game is flushed he is not tempted to run in and retrieve, but will sit and wait to be asked to retrieve.

Retrieving

The Straight Retrieve   Retrieving is the exercise we usually finish on when training a dog. He enjoys it so much it gives him a high note on which to finish the day's work.

Your new puppy will be happy and mentally stimulated by being able to retrieve for you. His first dummy, the carrying not the sucking variety, is ideal for this purpose. A sock stuffed with old tights is as good as anything. It is light and soft and a good shape to carry.

When he is older, you will need two or three dummies to use for training. The old socks will do initially, but later on you will find it best to purchase some. The commercially made ones are the right length and weight as well as being covered in canvas, making them very durable and economical. Experienced shooting and trialing folk often make their own to a specific shape and weight.

Never allow your dog to play with them, as in effect they are your game and must be respected at all times as such. He must learn the golden rule that the dummy must be retrieved for you carefully each time.

It is best to start with proper retrieves in familiar surroundings, but without any distractions. Show him your dummy. Sit him down at your side and hold on to him, because he will want to run off. Throw the dummy a short distance, make sure that he is interested in it and let him go. Say 'on and fetch' and encourage him forward. When he has the dummy call him back to you. He must be taught or conditioned always to fetch this prize – the dummy – and bring it back to you without fail. Don't be tempted to grab the dummy. If he thinks you are going to grab the dummy, he will instinctively bite harder to stop you, and he will develop a 'hard mouth' – a dreadful sin in a gundog.

When the dog brings you the dummy, encourage him by praising and stroking him, and restrain him from dashing off without releasing the dummy. Say 'dead' and hold your hand at his mouth, so that he will give the dummy to you. If he persists in hanging on to the dummy, put your first finger in the side of his mouth, where the gap between his teeth is, and wiggle it about to open his jaw. When his jaw is opened wide enough to release the dummy, catch it with your other hand, never pull it. Only repeat the exercise once or twice so that the process doesn't bore him. He should not be allowed to become complacent and to begin to treat the process like a game.

He may go through the stage of not returning the dummy to you, and may go off with it instead. Don't run after him. Call him, then turn and run away from him. This will worry him and he will follow you. Again praise him when he reaches you and after you have taken the dummy away from him.

Although he did it right in the end, it might be wise not to try any more retrieves that day, as this might precipitate a repeat performance. Far better to leave it for another day and start with a clean slate.

Another fault is for him to try to retrieve everything or indeed every dummy thrown. He must learn to retrieve only on command. A good way to do this is to make him sit and then throw a dummy. Leave him sitting and go and retrieve the dummy yourself. This teaches good control.

The Unseen Retrieve   Once you have mastered the straight retrieve, then you can go on to the unseen retrieve. Sit your dog, then throw the dummy over a low wall and ask him to 'on and fetch'. When he reaches the wall, encourage him with 'over'. If he falters at the obstacle, encourage him all the way. If necessary, go over the wall and encourage him from the other side. When he makes the retrieve call him back to you. If you have had to go over the wall, you will have to dash back to your original position and then call him back.

A wall is the best start to jumping; it is solid and not as off-putting nor as dangerous as a fence. Any introduction to a barbed wire fence is best achieved by covering it with something so that the dog doesn't tear himself going over it. I have always found that because Weimaraners are so athletic, they enjoy jumping over obstacles to retrieve.

Another unseen retrieve that proves useful is throwing the dummy into long grass. Because he has seen the dummy fall, your dog will have an idea where it lies. He will then have to rely on his nose to find the dummy. If you know where the dummy is encourage him forward, then when he is getting warm call 'hie lost' and he will begin to recognise he is close. When he finds the dummy, stop calling so that he can concentrate on the retrieve without distractions.

As you progress with retrieving, it is a good idea to fasten a pair of pheasant wings to the dummy. This gives him the idea that he is retrieving game.

You can then go a step further and retrieve cold, dead game. Pigeons are often used for this exercise. I have always found that their feathers come out very easily and can put the dog off. If you use pigeons it may be a good idea to tape the feathers to the body of the bird with elastic bands for a novice dog.

You should seek expert advice to progress further. However, this gives the basics to work with and you will be able to get out and start training your puppy until he is ready to attend classes.

The Water Retrieve   Something best learned from practical lessons is the water retrieve. It is useful to introduce your youngster to water beforehand so that class time is not wasted getting him into the water. Never force your dog into the water, but encourage him to gain confidence.

If yours is an only dog and he has no one to follow, don the waders and get in there yourself. He will usually follow to be with you.

A perfect dummy for water retrieves is an old washing-up bottle, sealed at the end and put in a sock. This will then float and be gripped easily.

Ch. Shalina Sky Diver retrieving from the water.

Remember to introduce your puppy to water in summer; the water is far warmer than winter water. The shock of the cold, or even frozen winter water, may put him off the job for life. I would also make sure that the first water your dog retrieves in is reasonably clean. Nothing can be more upsetting for a young dog than an evil-smelling, stagnant pool.

The Gun

If you are a novice, you are capable of doing irrevocable damage to a young dog by shooting a gun near him. It is far better to introduce your youngster to the sound with someone who is experienced. He might, for instance, fire a starting pistol from a distance, while you hold and quieten your dog on a lead. Your dog will gain confidence more quickly because he is with you. He will be unable to dash off and you will be on hand to comfort him.

At the sound of the shot, give him the command to sit, so that from the beginning he is conditioned to sit at the sound of gunfire. Running in is a major fault in competition work. Basically, this is when the dog does not listen to commands but lets his instinct take over when a shot is fired. Instead of sitting, he will run off, wanting to retrieve what has been shot.

Summary

With all of these early training exercises, you are actually channelling and enhancing his instincts. The Weimaraner is intelligent and has an excellent memory; he will learn from a repetitive action. His aim is to please you. If you lack patience and get cross with him, he won't want to train with you for fear of upsetting you, so if you are not in a good mood one day, forget training until another day when you are in a happier frame of mind.

Keep the training lessons short. That way you have more chance of keeping them sweet. The ultimate aim of these sessions is for you to have a biddable dog, who is capable of hunting and finding game, pointing that game for the gun, flushing on command, sitting to the shot and retrieving the game gently, back to the gun, on command.

Providing your dog has a good working instinct, with patience and determination, you will have a dog that is welcome on any shoot, and will be a credit to you and the breed at Field Trials. You will be advised when you are ready to enter Field Trials. Enthusiasm will abound from every quarter. Take the advice offered from these more experienced people.

Entering a Trial

If you enter a Trial before either of you is ready, you will end up having a very embarrassing day and most likely ruining several other competitors' day as well if your dog has been caught up in the excitement and runs in uncontrollably.

A Field Trial consists of twelve runners. People enter their dogs and all the names are put in a hat. The first twelve out of the hat have preference of running in the Trial. The draw, as this is called, is done in advance of the Trial and because of this, reserves are drawn in case a dog cannot attend. For instance, he may have an injury or a bitch may have come into season.

Societies give preference to members or particular breeds. Even so, there are usually more entrants than places and a ballot has to be held. You will therefore be depriving somebody of a run if you enter when you and your dog are not ready.

It is far better to attend as many Trials as possible as a spectator. You will learn exactly what is expected in a less embarrassing way. Just watching the well-trained dog exploiting his instincts is exciting and you will return to your own training, brimming with insight, eagerness, confidence and enthusiasm.

When attending a Field Trial, you must obey the official in charge. The one carrying the red flag is the one of most importance to the spectator. You must stay close to that person at all times. The flag is held so that the guns can see it, so that if a bird breaks in the direction of the flag, then the guns will refrain from shooting so as not to injure anyone.

Always make sure you arrive in good time. Make sure you find the correct place to be.

It is best not to leave the Trial before the end. But if you have to, you *must* have the permission of the Judge or Chief Steward. You must also check the safest return route to base. Check you don't return over ground in the line of fire or ground not yet shot over.

These rules also apply when you enter your first Field Trials. Make sure your dog is quiet or else he will be responsible for alerting the game. Check you have your whistles on you. It is also useful to have a supply of chocolate bars handy. They are instant energy for both you and your dog.

You will not be allowed to use a stick during your run. The judges will be more favourable to your performance if you use hand signals and whistles in preference to your voice.

The rules and regulations of a Field Trial are laid down by The Kennel Club. They are reproduced in various publications, primarily the *Kennel Club Year Book*. It is worth studying the rules, which will give you an inkling of what is expected.

You may not wish to trial at all, but instead go beating with your dog. All of this information will be useful in that environment as well.

9 Working Trials

Working Trials were designed for the 'Working Group' breeds. Within this group are the German Shepherd Dog or Alsatian, the Border Collie and the Giant Schnauser.

The Working Trial incorporates various exercises which lend themselves to the needs of a police dog and the abilities required by a dog working in the army. I feel that people whose enthusiasm is for Working Trials *and* Weimaraners are doing the breed a service by showing how versatile and adaptable it is.

One of the largest organisations connected with Working Trials is ASPADS (Associated Sheep, Police and Army Dog Society). This society was founded in 1924 and is nationwide. If your interest is in Working Trials, this organisation and its members will help encourage and give facilities for members to attend Trials within their area. The society was set up to support the interest in obedience and to advance dog training. Other clubs and societies do exist and will offer similar encouragement and facilities, but ASPADS is probably the most accessible for the novice.

The advantages of Working Trials for dogs with the correct aptitude are endless. One dog is capable of doing the work of a number of men. For instance, a dog's scenting ability enables him to find things quickly and efficiently. The dog has the capability of going over, under or through where man cannot reach. The dog can be trained to chase and stop a criminal. Therefore, a dog trained in the art of Working Trials is an asset to society in general. Of course, anything which promotes dogs in a good light in these days of anti-dog feelings is beneficial.

There is an idea among some Weimaraner owners and breeders that the gundog instinct of the breed should be preserved at all costs, but that Working Trials are to be avoided because they bring out qualities in a Weimaraner which are not, or should not, be typical of a gundog breed. A Weimaraner should be soft-mouthed and friendly, but he is a powerful dog with an extremely intelligent brain.

I feel that an ordinary member of the public should not try to train a Weimaraner to Police or Patrol Dog (P.D.) standard. In the hands of an experienced police dog handler or another qualified person, this is a different matter. That person is knowledgeably exploiting the dog's ability; a layperson might make the dog vicious.

Field Trial enthusiasts argue that the Weimaraner's instincts should be utilised but, as Working Trial enthusiasts state, there is neither enough ground in the British Isles nor enough Trials to work all Weimaraners. You can, however, stage a Working Trial on smaller grounds and without the specialist 'props', i.e. game, needed for a Field Trial.

Working Trials are also far better for a Weimaraner than pure obedience. The activity of the Weimaraner in both physical and mental terms makes him suited to Working Trials because he has to use his brain to work things out and is expected to do more than just the repetitive exercises required with obedience work, which he soon tires of.

Obedience is necessary because the dog must obey every command explicitly. He must also learn to evaluate the situation and use his instinct, for example, in locating a body or object. Obedience is not a word often used in Working Trials. Control of the dog is what Working Trial enthusiasts require.

Gwen Sowersby specialises in Working Trials and she has written the following piece for this chapter.

Training your Weimaraner for Working Trials

It is essential for good, sound, basic obedience that your dog is able to work to heel at normal, slow and fast pace off the lead, and he must sit close to your left leg when you come to a halt position.

Retrieve

Your Weimaraner should be able to retrieve any article that is required of him. This for many is a difficult task, and is complicated if you scold the dog when he is very young for picking up articles which he shouldn't, e.g. your best shoe or glove, etc. Many people grumble at the dog so that he gets the idea that whatever he carries is wrong. *Never* scold him for what is natural. *Never* snatch the article away; in a firm kind voice just say 'leave', applying slight pressure over his mouth, and praise him as soon as he gives it to you.

In Working Trials the dog has to go into a twenty-five yard square area and find four articles which have to be scented out and not seen by the eye. To start this exercise, put large articles in the square, let the dog see you doing this, then send him in to retrieve them and praise him for every one found. He will soon get the idea, and as he does, decrease the size of the articles gradually until they reach matchbox size. By this time your dog should be able to find the articles by smell. For this exercise use the command 'find'.

Ch. Monroes Ambition of
Westglade with his owner
Gwen Sowersby, scaling a
six-foot jump. (p. 146)

The Sendaway

The dog is required to run in a straight line until told to stop by the handler. To start off, train your dog to go to a hedge. To do this, walk up to the hedge with your dog, put a toy or coat down on the ground and tell his 'down'. Then walk back five yards with the dog, set him up and point to whatever is on the ground and command him: 'get on' or 'away'. At the same time run up with him, giving whatever command you have chosen, and when he reaches the article put him in the down position. Repeat this several times, then take your dog back to your starting point, set him up, point to the article and say 'get on' or 'away', and by then the dog should run to the article. At that point the handler shouts 'down' and he should drop. When he has mastered the exercise for a short distance, go back a few more yards and repeat it until the dog will go out happily for one hundred yards or more. *Never* call your dog back to you; go to him and praise him well.

Agility

The dog is required to negotiate a three-foot clear jump and a nine-foot long jump, neither of which he may touch. He must also scramble over a nine-foot scale jump and return on command.

All Weimaraners like doing this – they are rather like frogs – but they must be taught to jump properly. The three-foot clear jump is started at a foot high and increases to three feet. The command is 'up', and the dog has to stay on the other side until the handler picks him up. The long jump ends at nine feet. Start off with small jumps and the 'over' command and gradually build up to the required length.

To start off, get the dog going over the scale and back at four feet, then build up by three or four inches at a time until the full height of six feet is reached. When he is going over tell him to stay. This position can be a 'stand', 'sit' or 'down'. Watch him and see what he does: if he sits always tell him to sit, or if he stands, the same applies. Approach the scale, tell him 'up' to stay, and then call 'back' in a happy voice.

Tracking

The dog is required to follow a human scent for half a mile and recover any article which the track layer places on the track. I use only one method for this and I find it works without too much pressure on the dog. I show the dog his favourite toy or rag, the dog and handler watch me walk out about fifty yards, waving the article, and at the same time I drag a trail of tripe behind me. I put the article down, return to the handler and dog and then the dog is asked to 'track'. In most cases the smell of the tripe gets his nose down and off he goes to find his article.

Praise him and play with him. With practice the dog will soon learn to track without the aid of food. This is an exercise Weimaraners love.

Val O'Keefe demonstrating tracking with Ch. Fossana Bruno.

Increase your distance as he improves. When he is going well start to put right- and left-hand turns in, so at the end of his training he can do a half-mile track with no problems. In his early training the track is half an hour; it is increased to one and a half hours, then it goes up to three hours.

Stays

A two minute 'sit' is required in the C.D. Stake with the handler out of sight and a ten minute 'down' in all stakes, again with the handler out of sight. These two exercises can be the downfall of many dogs. The 'stays' are one of the most important, and the dog must stay in his position under all circumstances, regardless of weather conditions. Weimaraners hate the wet and wind, so it is most important that you train in bad weather.

To begin these two exercises, command your dog, then lead him by moving just your right leg then gradually bring up your left leg. If he moves you are there to correct him and, most important, do not leave him at any distance until he is rock steady. Increase the distance little by little, and increase the time until he can be left out of sight for two minutes in the 'sit' and ten minutes on the 'down'.

Working Trials are not won overnight – they require perseverance, praise and patience. Train every day, and at the end you have a willing and wonderful dog.

Working Trial Qualifications

This initial training gives you an insight into what will be expected of your dog. If you wish to compete in Working Trials, you should attend classes. This will be a social occasion as well as a training exercise and much can be gained.

As you and your dog improve at class, your confidence builds up and the thought of competition may appeal to you. The Kennel Club have various Working Trial qualifications you can achieve as you progress:

C.D. – Companion Dog
U.D. – Utility Dog
W.D. – Working Dog
T.D. – Tracking Dog
P.D. – Patrol Dog.

To achieve a Working Trial Certificate the dog must obtain at least seventy per cent marks, as indicated in the schedule of points. If eighty per cent or more marks are achieved, excellent will be awarded, for example, C.D. ex or Companion Dog excellent.

Important Weimaraners in Working Trials

Mrs Milward qualified her bitch Strawbridge Irene to be the first Weimaraner to gain an obedience Challenge Certificate in 1958. This team led the way in Working Trials by gaining the C.D. ex.

In 1976 Val O'Keefe's dog 'Panzer' qualified C.D. ex at the Championship Working Trials at Bridgend in Wales, taking a reserve place. With determined, clever training, he went on to gain his U.D. ex, W.D. ex, and, no mean feat, his T.D. Not content with this, he also gained four Challenge Certificates and four res Challenge Certificates in the show ring. In 1978 he gained his Field Trial qualifier to become Ch. Fossana Bruno, C.D. ex, U.D. ex, W.D. ex, and T.D. – the highest achieving Weimaraner at that time.

Gwen Sowersby bought a puppy from Mrs Joan Matuszewska destined to become Ch. Monroes Ambition of Westglade, C.D. ex, U.D. ex, and W.D. ex. 'Mr Harvey', as the dog is known, gained his first C.C. at Crufts in 1981 and that year he was Weimaraner of the Year in The Weimaraner Club of Great Britain competition. He was awarded this title again in 1982. Mr

Ch. Fossana Bruno C.D. ex, U.D. ex, W.D. ex, T.D. Not only brains but beauty.

The loyal aristocratic look is typified by Ch. Monroes Ambition of Westglade C.D. ex, U.D. ex, W.D. ex.

Bob Lynch's Ch. Reeman
Aruac C.D. ex, U.D. ex,
W.D. ex, T.D. ex, on the
edge of a loch.

Harvey lost out on his T.D. certificate because he would not 'speak' on command.

In Scotland, Bob Lynch has entered Working Trials pioneering the Weimaraners since 1980. His dog Ch. Reeman Aruac C.D. ex, U.D. ex, W.D. ex, T.D. ex, affectionately known as 'Brig', is Scotland's only full breed Champion and Britain's most qualified Weimaraner to date. He is also the only champion in the Gundog Group to qualify T.D. ex in the Working Trials.

Jenny Wilson's 'Max' became the first Working Trial Champion Weimaraner, with the title W.T. Ch. Ritisons Constellation C.D. ex, U.D. ex, W.D. ex, and T.D. ex. He also has the honour of being the first Working Trial Champion in Scotland for the last fourteen years in any breed.

Born in 1982, Max became Working Trial Champion before he was six years old. Since 1984 Max has won various awards, such as The Weimaraner Club of Great Britain Weimaraner of the Year in 1984 and runner-up in 1986 and 1987. He has won the Bruno trophy, the Scottish Working Trial Weimaraner of the Year and the trophy for a Scottish-based dog of any breed with the highest achievement in Working Trials of the year.

In 1970, Paul Dodd, a police dog handler, took on the Weimaraner Metpol Monroes Thor bred by that clever dog breeder Joan Matuszewska. Thor has really shown what a Weimaraner is capable of with the right handler.

Thor was taken into service in November 1970 as a puppy and was trained and operational from December 1971. An excellent 'street' dog he had many arrests to his name. A great ambassador for the breed and as a police dog, he took part in Police and Kennel Club Competition Trials. Indeed, in his first Kennel Club Trial, he obtained 197 points out of a possible 200 and won the Trial over 31 entrants of all breeds.

Thor was the first Weimaraner to qualify W.D. ex, and is the only Weimaraner to date to have qualified P.D. ex. When he was three years old he was awarded the Frederika Shield for the best dog in the man work tests at a Police Dog Trial, beating all the G.S.D.s. He competed many times at local level and represented the force at the National Police Dog Trials in 1978, finishing a creditable tenth.

He was a member of the central demonstration team and appeared at Crufts, The Royal Tournament and on the BBC's *Blue Peter* programme. Thor retired from duty in 1980 and died in 1984.

Metpol Monroes Thor U.D. ex, W.D. ex, P.D. ex, handled by police dog handler Paul Dodd. The first and only Weimaraner to qualify Police Dog excellent.

10 Ailments and Health Care

To keep your Weimaraner in good condition mentally and physically, remember to:

Feed him the correct diet, at regular intervals daily.

Keep his environment hygienic, washing his bedding and basket regularly and delousing when necessary.

Exercise him daily and discipline him with firmness and kindness.

Check his ears, teeth and nails regularly.

Make sure you devote some time to him alone.

Keep your vet's telephone number in an easily accessible place. The last thing you need to be doing in an emergency is hunting through a directory.

A thermometer can be a useful item to have in the medical chest. A healthy dog has a temperature of 101.5°F or 38.5°C. The temperature will rise from excitement, stress or exercise, so be careful when you take it. If he is listless, refuses food and generally acts out of character, it may be worth taking his temperature. Please remember that animal thermometers are for rectal use, and if used orally do not work.

The first thing to do after bringing your puppy home is to make an appointment with your vet. This is so that he can have a medical and you can be advised about inoculations. The vaccinations are usually administered at about eight, twelve and eighteen weeks; thereafter an annual booster is administered.

Inoculating your puppy is very important, as he will then be protected against Distemper, Hard Pad, Hepatitis and Leptospirosis. These diseases can and do kill, but modern vaccines offer great protection against them. You must vaccinate to avoid contamination, as all of these diseases are prevalent throughout the country and are highly contagious.

In 1978 a new disease, Parvo Virus, became known. It is highly infectious and, more often than not, fatal. The young and old are especially susceptible to it, but dogs of all ages are at risk. Inoculations for this are administered at the same time as the others. You must take your vet's advice on all inoculations. You will not be saving yourself any money by not having them done if you lose your dog!

Common Diseases and Ailments

Burns

If your dog is burned, put cold water on the burn immediately to take out the heat. Shock may set in later, so keep him quiet, warm and comfortable. If the injury is severe contact your vet.

Constipation

If your dog is constipated, make sure you are feeding a sensible and balanced diet. Too many bones may cause constipation. If the problem persists, add a little bran to his food, or a dessert spoon of Liquid Paraffin may cure the problem. If the problem persists consult your vet. Don't let the problem drag on as the animal may well have an intestinal blockage.

Cryptorchidism

Another problem, which is hereditary, is Cryptorchidism. When this occurs the dog's testicles are retained in the abdomen or in the inquinal canal, the passage down which the testicle travels to descend into the scrotum. The general thought is that if both testicles are retained, then the dog is sterile and unable to sire puppies, However, a monorchid, where only one testicle is retained, can sire puppies, but it is obviously best to refrain from using such a dog at stud.

Testicles are suspended in the scrotum, which is outside the body, as the ideal temperature for storing sperm is lower than actual body temperature. If one or both testicles are retained, sperm can be destroyed by overheating and also may lead to disease and often cancer of the testicles. It is therefore wise to consult your vet if your dog's testicles have not descended by about six months of age. He will be able to assess what course of action is necessary.

Usually an operation to remove the testicles is performed to prevent future trouble. If the operation is performed on a monorchid dog, it may be advisable to have the normal testicle removed as well. This removes all risk of the dog siring puppies.

Castration will pose no problem for the dog, it tends to be the owner that suffers from the ethics of it. Dogs lead normal, healthy and happy lives after castration. Boredom and weight gain are not side effects of the operation, but are due to overfeeding, lack of exercise and understimulation.

Cystitis

Cystitis is as common in dogs as humans. The symptoms are discharge, traces of blood in urine, loss of bladder control and the need to empty the bladder far more frequently. It may be due to infection, but can also be caused by a growth or kidney stones. It will not rectify itself – treatment is always required. Special care is needed if a bitch in whelp is suffering from it, so consult your vet as soon as possible.

Diarrhoea

There is a fine line between going to the vet too soon and leaving a problem to develop into something major, so use your instincts and if in doubt see your vet. Diarrhoea is a condition which can have you dashing to the vet's without weighing up the whys and wherefores.

Diarrhoea can occur for a number of reasons, not all of them serious. Your dog may have eaten something that was rotten and decaying, or you may have changed his diet. In any event it is wise to starve him for twenty-four hours, but make sure he drinks plenty of liquid; if necessary, force-feed him spoonfuls at a time. Dehydration is by far the most serious consequence of diarrhoea. There should be no cause for alarm, but if after twenty-four hours he is still suffering symptoms, consult your vet.

Kaolin and Morphine are a useful addition to the medical chest. They treat minor tummy upsets wonderfully. Vomiting, high temperature, blood-stained and sloppy stools may be a sign of viral or bacterial infection. Your dog will need specialist treatment so pay a visit to your vet.

Entropion

A hereditary condition which is known to occur in some blood lines of Weimaraners is Entropion. This is distressing rather than dangerous to the dog. However, it is best not to breed from a dog suffering from it. The eyelashes of the dog are inverted, therefore causing them to rub on the dog's eyes making them sore and watery. A corrective operation is possible, which enables the dog to lead a normal life.

Fits

Fits can often be suffered by an older dog in a stressful situation, or there may be a hereditary problem. If this is the case the animal should not be bred from. The animal's breeder should also be informed, so that he can research the animal's lines for a history of such an illness.

If your dog has a fit he will collapse, his jaw will clamp and he will go rigid. There is often frothing at the mouth and he may empty his bladder and bowels. His legs may paddle and he might twitch. It is all very distressing to witness. Monitor him until he settles and comes out of the fit, which can take as long as thirty minutes. When he recovers, his eyes may be glazed, he might not know where he is and he might be confused. Keep him quiet and reassure him. Unless you are positive it is a fit, i.e. by previous diagnosis, consult your vet.

Gastric Torsion

Weimaraners are known to suffer from the complaint known as Gastric Torsion. Because the Weimaraner is a deep-chested, long-backed, big breed, he is more prone to Gastric Torsion than some other breeds.

The dog becomes restless and starts suffering stomach pains. He will then start to retch and try to vomit, and his stomach will start to swell. You must take him to a vet immediately to increase the chance of saving him. The vet will probably insert a tube into the stomach to release the built-up gases, relieving the pressure and preventing the torsion or stomach twisting.

However, once the intestine has twisted the gases build up and the stomach distends, rather like a balloon. This puts pressure on other organs, further complications arise and an immediate operation is necessary. Even if he does survive the operation, shock can and often does lead to his eventual death.

No one really knows why Gastric Torsions occur. Consequently we always feed Weimaraners twice daily. We also avoid strenuous exercise immediately before and after a meal, and we do not allow an over-thirsty dog unlimited water. However, a dog may suffer a torsion despite these precautions.

Haematoma

Sometimes, especially in young, fast-growing Weimaraner puppies, a soft lump on the occipital bone may develop. This is known as a Haematoma. It is quite common in more active breeds of dog and is caused by the animal banging his head on something. It can be quite large and very unsightly. Left alone it will generally go away; surgery can often result in unnecessary complications. The lump consists of fluid, as a cushion to protect the injury, which, if drained, will often fill up again. Left alone it will disperse naturally, but it may take a number of weeks.

Heart Attack

An older dog may begin to cough if he develops heart trouble. An actual heart attack has the symptoms of a sudden collapse and the dog may even appear to be dead. He will generally revive after a few minutes. During his blackout he may involuntarily open his bowels and empty his bladder, and

A Haematoma on the
occipital bone. (p. 155)

his eyes may rotate upwards. When he recovers sufficiently, seek your vet's
advice.

Hip Dysplacia

Another hereditary problem which can occur in Weimaraners is Hip
Dysplacia (HD). This condition is a malformation of the hip joint. If
sufficiently severe the dog can suffer considerable pain when standing up.
He will also tire easily and appear lame. A dog may be thought to have Hip
Dysplacia purely because his hindquarters look weak, or he has an unusual
gait. However, this may be due to bad construction; he may be straight in
the stifle or cow hocked and neither condition has anything to do with Hip
Dysplacia.

Hip Dysplacia can be very distressing for the dog and his owner. Good
breeders are careful not to breed from stock with bad hip scores to try and
reduce the problem (see below). However, as it is not purely a hereditary
problem, we cannot eradicate it by breeding alone. Environmental elements
may also be a factor and these can occur with even the most carefully bred
dog.

The Kennel Club runs a scheme in conjunction with the British
Veterinary Association, whereby a dog, usually of one year or over, can have
an X-ray taken by a vet which will show if the dog is suffering from Hip
Dysplacia.

A panel of experts scrutinise the plates and each hip is scored as to the
degree of Hip Dysplacia it has. 0–0 is the ideal score and means the dog is

free from the problem. Any other score shows that the dog is suffering from the complaint and to what degree. If the problem is slight and will cause the animal no problems, the breeder may decide to breed from the dog or bitch.

If the animal is in severe pain, the vet may decide to remove the offending hip joint. Gristle then forms and because bone is no longer rubbing on bone the pain is removed and the dog is once more able to enjoy life. Obviously this is an extreme measure and every care should be taken to prevent the problem from occurring.

Kennel Cough

Kennel Cough is a disease which can be inoculated against. Many boarding kennels insist on this vaccination before a dog is allowed to board with them. This is because Kennel Cough is an airborne virus and therefore highly contagious. If only one dog in the kennel has it, you can guarantee that before he leaves every dog will be infected.

Its symptoms are similar to those of the common cold in humans and it is treated in a similar fashion. Benilyn can be administered to relieve a sore throat and aspirin for a headache. The infected dog generally appears to suffer more at night, especially if he is in a stuffy room. If his symptoms worsen, consult your vet, as complications can set in, in the form of Bronchitis or Pneumonia.

Lumps and Bumps

Mammary Lumps   Mammary lumps may form on or around bitches' teats and these must be examined by your vet. Some lumps are benign while others are malignant. If in doubt don't ignore them, seek professional advice; you may save your dog's life.

You have to weigh up the pros and cons of surgery in an old dog though. You may consider it kinder to let an old dog live until his time is up if he is not in pain or discomfort.

Sebaceous Cysts   Older dogs may start to develop a variety of lumps and bumps. Sebaceous Cysts are not uncommon in Weimaraners and with their smooth coat are easily seen. These are often best left alone unless they start to grow or cause discomfort. They are usually the size of a marble and are not attached to the muscle, but to the skin. If they are attached to the muscle they may well be something more serious and your vet must examine them.

Parasites

Skin problems are not particularly common with Weimaraners. If a sore red patch breaks out, check that it is not caused by parasites. They may cause the dog to chew and scratch his skin, causing inflammation.

Fleas   Don't be shocked if you find fleas: they can and do affect the most well-cared-for and clean dogs. Fleas are common, but can be difficult to spot. Fortunately Weimaraners are very short haired, so it is not too difficult to find them if they are there. They should be checked for regularly. If your dog is biting himself and scratching incessantly, then you should check his coat immediately. Remember fleas move very quickly. They may leave brown droppings in the coat, and these droppings, which are generally easier to see, are usually behind the ears, down the back and under the armpits.

Don't bother with over-the-counter remedies, but seek your vet's advice. He will have the safest and most effective remedial preparations. Fleas lay eggs in the coat so a second treatment may be required. Your vet may prescribe a lotion, spray or powder, all of which are effective and safe if used correctly. Remember to treat the dog's basket, household carpets, chairs and anything the dog is in contact with. This is usually done with a spray and protects the home for roughly six weeks.

Fleas are generally most prevalent when the weather is warm and wet, our usual summer. As they are one of the intermediate hosts of the common canine tapeworm, it is wise to be vigilant about them.

Harvest Mites   Harvest mites are usually found in the ears and between the toes; treatment is similar to the treatment for fleas. If they are present in the ear, the dog will scratch and shake his head. The vet will give you drops for his ears. This violent shaking of the head can easily cause Haematoma of the ear.

Irritations   It is worth mentioning that too rich a diet may cause scratching. Household cleaning products can also cause irritations.

A puppy may be allergic to all sorts of plants and grasses in his first spring and summer. We have experienced this, but have found that the dog naturally becomes immune to such allergies in time and they never recur.

Lice   Lice are small, slow-moving insects, most often found on the inside of the thighs, leg joints and ears. The treatment for them is the same as for fleas.

Mange   Mange is caused by several kinds of mite. Treatment is usually a wash prescribed by your vet and carefully administered as they can be very nasty.

Sheep Ticks   Sheep ticks are sucking parasites and attach themselves to the host by burrowing their head into the skin and then sucking blood from the animal. They are easily seen – look for slate-grey appendages the size of a small wart. You can remove them by placing the nail of your thumb and forefinger behind their heads and jerking them out. Be careful not to leave the head behind or it can cause problems. Another way to remove them is by soaking a pad of cotton wool in methylated or surgical spirit and holding it over them for a few minutes to cause them to drop off.

People have been known to burn them off with a cigarette, but this is highly precarious and potentially painful. If all else fails insecticide spray should do the trick.

Poison

The taking of poison by dog or human is serious and frightening. Weimaraners can be poisoned through eating poisoned rodents, foxes or rabbits. If human medicine or garden weedkillers are carelessly stored, they may be ferreted out by your dog and consumed. If poisoning is suspected seek veterinary advice immediately. If possible, a sample of the suspect substance should be taken along with you, so that it can be verified. Symptoms of poisoning are vomiting, collapse or bleeding. Do not hesitate to go to the vet.

Worms

Internal parasites are generally known as worms. You must always be aware and vigilant about them. They are controlled fairly easily and if all dog owners wormed regularly and acted responsibly the anti-dog brigade would have no cause for complaint.

All dogs have worms but they can be kept under control by worming regularly every six months. A variety of potions can be purchased over the counter, but again I would advise you to ask your vet. He will find the one best suited to you and your dog.

A bitch carries dormant larvae in muscle tissue, which are activated by certain hormones present when she is pregnant. The puppies are then infected through the placenta. All puppies are born infected with worms to varying degrees and should be wormed from about three weeks of age. Again, the relevant advice and medicine should be sought from your vet.

Worms can be picked up fairly easily by adult dogs. The eggs are excreted in the faeces. The dog can gain access to the egg by eating the lice, lice fleas or rodents, all of which are intermediate hosts to the larvae. The eggs hatch, the larvae develop into adult worms, which in turn lay more eggs.

Hook and Whip Worms   Hook and Whip Worms are uncommon but can occur. They are not visible to the naked eye. If they are suspected, a sample of the dog's faeces must be sent for testing. A general sign of infection is loss of condition and debility.

Ringworm   The name ringworm suggests an infestation of burrowing worms, but it is in actual fact a fungal infection. It is highly contagious to both man and beast. It appears as a raised, angry red lump. If left untreated the infection will spread.

Round Worm   British dogs are most commonly troubled by the Round Worm, Ascarid or the *Toxocara canis*. It is the egg from the latter which if swallowed by a human can develop and cause blindness. Children are most likely to swallow the egg if they have been playing around ground recently fouled by a dog. The chance of a child being infected is roughly two million to one, but no one should be responsible for such a disaster just by neglecting to worm his dog regularly.

Tapeworm   Tapeworm is not as prevalent, but can certainly be contracted, usually by an adult dog. A dog walking on farmland where sheep and rabbit droppings can be eaten, can be infected by the tapeworm. Again, fleas, lice and rodents are intermediate hosts of the worm. Tapeworms are very long, and are made up of several segments of about half an inch each. The segments break off and are passed out in the dog's motions. They can appear as small white grain-like particles, rather similar in appearance to long grain rice. You must make sure that the head of the worm is passed out as well, because if it is not removed by treatment it will grow again. Your vet will prescribe the relevant cure; make sure you follow his instructions.

Wounds

Because this breed is so active and has such a fine coat, cuts and tears of the coat are common. If such damage occurs, try to treat it without stitches if possible. Do this by bathing it in salt water often and maybe dusting it with wound powder. This is because healthy dogs' skin generally heals well and quickly. If a wound is stitched a collar has to be worn to prevent the dog tearing the stitches and causing more damage. If you have more than one dog he has to be separated from the others so they don't play and damage the wound further. If in doubt consult your vet and follow his advice.

After an Accident   Accidents are a hazard of all life. If your dog is in a traffic accident or is badly hurt, try and keep calm, for his sake as well as yours. If at all possible take him to your vet's surgery; the surgery is the best place to have the dog treated as the vet has all he requires to hand. If this is not possible then the vet will make a house call. If the animal is bleeding badly apply a pressure pad or tourniquet, but be careful not to leave it on too long or it will cut off the circulation.

If you have to move him, do it with care so as not to cause further damage and stress. A useful way to move a hurt animal is to ease him on to a blanket or coat, so that when he is lifted undue pressure is not applied to a damaged area.

If he is in pain, don't kiss and cuddle him as your instinct would dictate. His pain may lead him to bite you. If he is snarling it may be best to try to bandage or muzzle his mouth. Remember not to crowd him, but gently reassure him until professional help is there.

Bites Animal bites, usually from other dogs, are another major cause of distress to you and your dog. Bathe the wound in salt water, but watch deep puncture wounds as they may become infected or develop an abscess. Severe bites of any kind should be looked at by your vet, as should any bite caused by a rodent, because of the number of diseases rodents carry.

Everybody has their own personal 'pet cure-all', mine is salt. Salt is an antiseptic substance, which draws infection and promotes healing. It may sting a little, but the benefits outweigh the drawbacks. Soothe your dog with words of love, and persevere. Just remember not to use too strong a saline solution and use it often.

Snake bites are also a possibility in some areas. The adder is the only poisonous snake that is a natural resident of Britain. Your vet should be consulted immediately and if possible a tourniquet should be applied in the meantime to prevent venom from circulating in the bloodstream.

Care of the Weimaraner

In general Weimaraners are a very healthy breed and the worst they usually suffer is an odd cut or knock, due mostly to their natural exuberance. They remain active and healthy looking, well into old age. They also remain mentally active.

To keep your dog in such good condition, you need good animal husbandry and a certain amount of luck. Normal common-sense care in checking anal glands, coat, ears, over-long nails and teeth will help keep your Weimaraner happy and your vet's bills down.

Anal Glands

Anal glands can cause problems if not cared for. They are situated at either side of the anus and are there for the purpose of secreting a lubricant which helps the faeces of the dog to be passed more easily.

If the dog has been badly frightened he may accidentally release the contents of the glands. If it splashes on your clothes, they will need lots of washing as it is a most foul-smelling substance.

The anal glands may become full and blocked on occasion, they then have to be emptied manually. If this is done at home, remember to do it outside. Ask someone to hold the dog still while you lift his tail.

It may be wise to wear thin surgical gloves, obtainable from your chemist, but at least to have some tissue wrapped over your hand to catch the fluid. With your thumb and forefinger at twenty past and twenty to the hour at each side of the anus, gently squeeze up, expelling the contents of the glands. Make sure they are totally empty, because leaving any liquid may result in infection. In extreme cases of infection the glands may have to be removed surgically. This leaves the dog able to manage quite nicely without the help of the lubricant. A dog may appear out of condition, with lifeless eyes and yet as soon as his glands are evacuated his whole condition improves dramatically.

Coat

The coat of a Weimaraner is short, smooth and sleek. Moulting does occur but not profusely. It certainly does not cause the problems of a moulting Labrador.

The beauty of his coat is highlighted by the fact that you can exercise him over a muddy field only to find that with a couple of shakes the mud has dropped off. If he is out in the rain, he will dry without leaving an awful wet dog odour.

Your hand is as good as anything for grooming him. The oil in your hand is enough to create a good sheen, or you may find a chamois leather is useful for promoting a good gloss on the coat. The types of rubber curry combs and body brushes used on horses are also very effective. They not only remove caked mud but they also stimulate the circulation of the hair follicles. A rubber glove or a small piece of old tyre is also very effective for grooming and is especially useful if the dog is moulting, as the rubber draws the hair out quite miraculously.

It may be necessary for a bath to be administered once in a while – not too often though as this serves to remove all the natural oils from the coat that keep it healthy and shiny. You may often find that a dog who is quite happy to swim all day in foul, freezing lake water may not take too kindly to the warm water of the bathtub, very like small boys. It may therefore be easier to train him to the idea of baths while young and small enough to be handled easily if he objects strongly. If you do it properly he might even begin to enjoy a bath, but if not at least he will have realised that there isn't much he can do about it and endure the procedure gracefully.

Wet him all over, then shampoo his face, but be careful not to allow water or shampoo in his ears. Rinse the head thoroughly, trying not to drip anything into his eyes. Use a good shampoo, either for dogs or humans. Shampoo may not harm his eyes, but it will alienate him to the whole procedure.

Next, lather his body, taking special care with his armpits and all his important little places. Be careful around his tail as, for some reason, a dog can suffer 'dead tail' the day after a bath. The tail when lifted sticks out at the root then drops. The dog has no control over it at all, it simply hangs. It can be quite painful if touched. However, it does clear up after a day and affords the dog no permanent injury.

Rinse the dog thoroughly or the shampoo may cause irritation or dandruff. A chamois leather is ideal for taking excess water out of the coat, which will then dry naturally. Don't let the dog get cold after a bath, as he is definitely more susceptible to chills at such times. If you are bathing him for entering a show, I would advise you to do it a couple of days beforehand. This allows time for the natural oils to return to his coat, giving him a far better appearance.

Ears

Ears can harbour foul smells if not looked after properly. Caution is needed however. Do not on any account poke around in ears indiscriminately, as you will surely cause more harm than good.

A proprietary solution can be obtained from your vet, complete with instructions. A few drops are placed in the ear, you then externally massage the ear to work the drops in. With pads of cotton wool you wipe away the resulting debris, leaving the ear clean. Don't use ear buds as you may inadvertently prod too deeply into the inner ear and cause injury.

Weimaraners are not as prone to ear problems as some breeds are. Regular sensible attention is generally all that is needed.

However, if your dog shakes his head a lot or starts to scratch his ear, then he may have developed an ear mite. They are virtually undetectable, but can cause great discomfort and problems. Too much head shaking and scratching of the ear may cause Haematoma of the ear – the blood vessels in the ear flap burst, due to extreme head shaking. The cure is usually an operation, in which the ear is strapped to the side of the head to prevent the head shaking. Prevention is a lot better than cure. If nothing is done, the swelling will reduce and will, in time, leave the ear stiff and curled.

Weimaraners do tend to tear or nick the ear, which bleeds profusely. Because his ears are fine and reasonably long in length, the dog catching them on things can be a recurring problem. Potassium Permanganate crystals can help stop the bleeding, but it may also be wise to bandage the ear to the head for a short while as well. This prevents him shaking his head and ear, and starting the bleeding again just as the ear is healing.

Nails

Long nails are a particular problem with Weimaraners, because they tend to play with their front legs and long nails can leave terrible marks on humans and other animals.

As a breed their nails are clear, which means they can be cut quite safely and easily. Specialist nail clippers do have to be used, and these can be bought quite cheaply. There is no need to have an expensive pair.

I find the best type of nail clippers are those resembling round-bladed scissors, with an indentation in each blade, forming a hole to hold the nail. They are better because both blades cut the nail simultaneously. The guillotine-type clippers cut with one blade as the other blade squeezes from the other side. This may be the cause of some discomfort for the dog.

You should cut as close as possible to the edge of the quick. If you get too close the nail will bleed quite a lot. You can buy crystals which are dabbed on the nail to stop the bleeding effectively.

If the nail is cut regularly the quick stays short. If the nails are rarely cut then the quick tends to grow long, making it impossible to cut the nail short without an expensive operation at the vet's. The dog is anaesthetised and the nails clipped back hard, making them very short. The nail bleeds and has to be cauterised – an altogether uncomfortable procedure for the dog.

The dog becomes used to having his nails clipped if it is done regularly right from the start. Most Weimaraners hate having their nails cut, but if they are used to it, they will accept it as an unpleasant, but normal part of their life.

Teeth

Teeth are obviously very important to a dog, especially to a large working gundog whose purpose in life includes retrieving.

Gums need looking after just as much as teeth and one of the best ways to achieve this is to give your dog something sensible to chew. Chewing is essential from an early age, as it helps massage the gums, achieves a good supply of blood and exercises the jaw. In time it helps with the removal of milk teeth, allowing the permanent teeth to erupt normally. With healthy jaws and gums, you have the basis for healthy teeth.

We need to make a conscious effort to promote healthy teeth and gums. This is not simply a matter of providing the necessary raw bones. It has been proved that domestic dogs do not have the depth of enamel on their teeth that wild dogs do. A continuous supply of bone could, therefore, be more

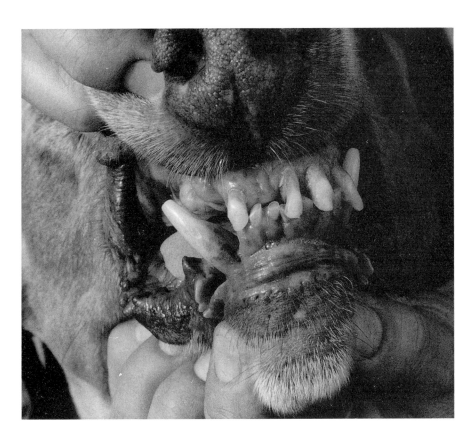

damaging than no bone at all, by eroding the enamel and exposing the core of the teeth. Such erosion of the teeth is unacceptable in the show ring, and of course for the future health of the dog.

As with humans, some dogs have exceptionally strong teeth, which never require any treatment and others have softer teeth, which may need care and attention to maintain them in good condition. Cleaning of the teeth can be done at home with a soft toothbrush. Dog toothpaste, with appealing flavours for your dog, can be purchased from your vet. They are expensive however. An alternative is to dip the brush in salt, which will remove all plaque and bacteria from the teeth.

If the tartar has built up and you cannot remove it yourself, it can be removed by scaling, which is done under an anaesthetic by your vet. If tartar is not removed, as with humans, gum disease can result, leading to the loss of some teeth. Disease in gums and teeth can and does lead to various other maladies: bad breath, for instance.

Ultimately this care should lead to a very healthy Weimaraner, who will enjoy a long and happy life as a member of your family.

This dog had a gum disease which caused the gums to recede and bacteria to affect the teeth. Numerous teeth were removed and others have loosened.

Index

Numbers in italics refer to photographs